Souls Are Made
of Endurance

Also by Stewart D. Govig
and published by
Westminster John Knox Press

Strong at the Broken Places:
Persons with Disabilities
and the Church

Souls Are Made of Endurance

---

*Surviving Mental Illness
in the Family*

Stewart D. Govig

Westminster John Knox Press
Louisville, Kentucky

Scripture quotations from the New Revised Standard Version of the Bible are copyright © 1989 by the Division of Christian Education of the National Council of the Churches of Christ in the U.S.A. and are used by permission.

Grateful acknowledgment is made to copyright holders for the use of the following material.

"Do Not Go Gentle into That Good Night," by Dylan Thomas, from *Collected Poems, 1934–52,* published by J. M. Dent & Sons, London, and New Directions, Inc., New York. Used by permission of David Higham Associates and New Directions, Inc.

"Take Up Your Cross," by Carl Sandburg, used by permission of Rosenman & Colin, New York.

Book design by Drew Stevens

Cover design by Peyton Tabb Talbott III

First edition

Published by Westminster John Knox Press
Louisville, Kentucky

This book is printed on acid-free paper that meets the American National Standards Institute Z39.48 standard. ∞

PRINTED IN THE UNITED STATES OF AMERICA

94 95 96 97 98 99 00 01 02 03 —10 9 8 7 6 5 4 3 2 1

Library of Congress Cataloging-in-Publication Data

Govig, Stewart D. (Stewart Delisle), date.
    Souls are made of endurance: surviving mental illness in the
family / Stewart D. Govig. — 1st ed.
        p.   cm.
    Includes bibliographical references.
    ISBN 0–664–25289–3 (acid-free paper)
    1. Mentally ill—Family relationships—Case studies.
2. Schizophrenics—Family relationships—Case studies.   3. Mentally
ill—Family relationships—Religious aspects—Christianity.
I. Title.
RC455.4.F3G68   1994
362.2′042—dc20   94–8688

For Alice

Soul Mate

Take up your cross, and go
the thorn way.

And if a sponge of vinegar be
passed you on a spear,

Take that too. Souls are made
of endurance.

God knows.

Carl Sandburg
(unpublished piece from
a notebook of 1902)

Contents

Preface

At a convention of the Association of Mental Health Clergy in Chicago, I was approaching the end of my paper, "Dark Side of the Dream" when, to my astonishment, my tears interrupted the concluding sentences. My halting effort to finish was mixed with applause from the priests, rabbis, and ministers in the room. Two years afterward, one of them remembered the episode: "My God, I thought, this guy is getting therapy here!" True enough. It was the first time I had tried to speak in public about our family's experience with mental illness.

When the journal *Word and World* announced plans to devote a 1989 issue to the subject, I decided to rewrite the Chicago paper for submission since I felt a personal witness would be important to their effort. Thus "Wilderness Journal: Parental Engagement with Young Adult Mental Illness" came about. The result was dramatic. Phone calls and letters arrived from across the country. At conferences came handshakes and hugs. A mother whose daughter has schizophrenia said, "I read it every three months or so and weep."

It must have struck a nerve. At the end of the piece I stated that we had seen "the banks of the Jordan," a metaphor to suggest that we have accepted our son's devastating illness and, in some fashion, over-come it. But what next? What happens when you cross over into the Promised Land? (Israel learned to live on edge.) How do you live with a long-term illness like this one? *Souls Are Made of Endurance* portrays one family's experience. I have sought words to lessen the burden of outrageous injustice borne by these most vulnerable and underserved citizens of our land—those with mental illness—and at the same time to cultivate hope in the face of caregiver overload.

Dr. Lewis Judd, director of the National Institute of Mental Health (NIMH), recently reported how our society continues to treat mental illnesses as though they were not as important as other illnesses; in fact, NIMH research funds are down. The statistics are startling: Schizophrenia is *five times* more common than multiple sclerosis and *six times* more prevalent than insulin-dependent diabetes; it is *sixty times* more common than muscular dystrophy. *One in five* Americans will have a mental disorder at some time in life. One reason for the neglect is the myth of permanent affliction; but in fact, people can and do recover.[1]

At the 1990 American Psychiatric Association national convention in New York, I heard psychiatrists examining "spirituality" and the emerging potential for more cooperation with religious communities. Additional discussions came out in a publication later that year. On the one hand, clergy (pastoral counselors) acknowledge the need for persons with psychiatric expertise to diagnose and treat severely dis-turbed individuals. Medical professionals, on the other, recognize how the confines of a mental health facility limit their access to a client's personal bonds of family, neighborhood, and, in some cases, church. In caregiving, then, each type of specialist participates in a different resource network. Based on a number of interviews with psychiatrists, one observer notes their desire for developing a better collaboration with potential caregiver groups such as colleges and re-ligious congregations. Most psychiatrists felt disappointed in the fail-ure of respected pastoral colleagues to engage the resources of reli-gious reality. In their view, issues of patient management, biology, and psychodynamics were not enough. Patients who confide in clergy about fears and anxieties, they argue, should not end up getting psy-chotherapy at the expense of an exploration of spiritual values.[2]

My survey of spirituality amplifies the personal witness intention of the "Wilderness Journal" article. In *The Minimal Self* the historian and social critic Christopher Lasch analyzes what he terms a "survival mentality." Media exposure of the troubled times of various individuals has promoted "victim" awareness. Tales of survival despite great odds to the contrary can even promote a notion of the survivor's moral superiority.[3] More recently, Robert Hughes' *Culture of Complaint* cites the concept of victim as hero; cult therapies suggest that "dysfunctional" families produce victims. Further, by complaining about such a situation, the heroic casualty may achieve emotional bribery power sufficient to create previously unnoticed levels of social guilt.[4] Rejecting both victim and hero ideas, I prefer persuasion and a search for truth. I hope people will understand more about the consequences of mental illness in the family, some of which it would be easier to remain silent about.

"Watch with me" (or "stay awake"), Jesus asked his disciples in the Garden of Gethsemane (Matt. 26:38). Rather than "Discover with me" or "Explain this crisis," I interpret his call as "Witness with your presence here." To unravel what I mean, in *Souls Are Made of Endurance* I try to downplay the language of popular psychology and give preference to theological thought. My search for reality on a pilgrimage of faith envisions God at work *sustaining* as well as healing and restoring.[5]

The notes at the end of the book contain the titles of resource books and articles on the subject of serious mental illness and the family. Most of them focus on the acute stage; moreover, few, if any, give space to spiritual or "religious reality" concerns. In addition, seldom is the chronic or long-term situation addressed. Thus, in these pages I cite both contexts for promising conversation possibilities. To proposals for increased psychosocial family training, I add my plea for religious education.

In this account, the names of family members, the state hospital, and the two private institutions with psychiatric wards have been changed.

The learning context I have in mind is built on two foundations. The first is the Bible. The texts I cite are not intended to form a spiritual psychology of adapting; rather, for me they shape a caregiver spirituality and a living voice of endurance.

Personal anecdotes form the other base. These brief sketches cover a span of approximately fifteen years. Since in all the confusion I kept no detailed diary or journal, they are marshaled only in rough chronological order. Several are culled from hospital records, but most surfaced from a storehouse of indelible memory. Reminiscence enhances research; at the same time ambiguities and questions remain open-ended. I take stories of personal struggle—such as in cases of mental disorder—not merely as illustrations of suffering. They can become vehicles for rebirth and hope. To conclude that all the heart-aches we as a family met, endured, and still live with have no point at all would complete a circle of cruelty. Stories are weapons to break bonds of fear and despair; accounts from witnesses shape the truth required to overcome the flow of angry tears. There is life after schizophrenia, clinical depression, and bipolar disorder.

"All happy families are like one another," asserts Leo Tolstoy, but "each unhappy family is unhappy in its own way."[6] The claim, I suspect, falls short: Unhappy families (self-declared) can become like one another, too. "Blessed are the poor in spirit," Jesus said (Matt. 5:3); in recent years, I have come to read a personal variation into the words: "Blessed are those at the end of their resources." This is the way it is when you share the life of a loved one whose brain reels from the foreign genes, chemicals, or other stresses that jump-start a crucial body organ to go to war against itself. The aftermath journey surely must qualify spouse, parent, and child for whatever the Master meant by "poor in spirit."

I feel a kinship here with parents of children who are developmentally disabled. We recognize aversion and stigma. One of them has written her story and I am indebted to her work, *Some Just Clap Their Hands*, for the three section titles of my narrative.[7]

The first of these, "Finding Out," deals with difficulties surrounding the diagnosis of a case of major mental illness; the second, "Holding On," enters the context of treatment; the final division, "Letting Go," explores rehabilitation potentials. Religious reality and spiritual values are linked to confession of vulnerability and Faith in part 1. The chapters in part 2, "Holding On," support dimensions of self-forgiveness and Hope. Part 3 adds the forgiveness of others with the scriptural counterpart of Love (1 Corinthians 13).

The poor in spirit are also blessed, proclaims Jesus, for "theirs is the kingdom of heaven." This is also the way it is when you get to the end of your resources. Rebirth surprises, and you begin to observe life and people in a new way: Prior innocence and bankruptcy stand un-masked.

This book, then, is about a family both happy and unhappy. A sponge of vinegar has become rich food for the soul. God knows.

Acknowledgments

I owe much to those who have guided an inspired me in preparing this book. At Westminster John Knox Press, Alexa Smith encouraged me to start writing; further along, Harold Twiss and Carl Helmich made many valuable suggestions for improving the manuscript.

Fred B. Craddock of Emory University brought the Carl Sandburg poem to my attention in a printed sermon, and Warren R. Weber, Acting Superintendent of the Carl Sandburg Home National Historic Site, helped track it down.

I want to thank Dennis Busse of the Evangelical Lutheran Church in America's Disabilities Ministry Office and George Doebler of the Association of Mental Health Clergy, denominational colleagues in the field. H. Newton Malony of Fuller Seminary and Jennifer Shifrin of Pathways to Promise have assisted me and others to go public with our burdens.

Duane Glasscock, head of the NAMI Religious Outreach Network together with Kaye Olsen, Pastors Phil Petrasek, and Paul Reitmann have opened my eyes to possibilities for ministry here in the Puget Sound area. I thank Gene for his encouragement and Marion for her prayers. The good humor of Chaplain Harvey Berg has revealed healing surprises in the effort to lighten up amid anxious moments of care.

ACKNOWLEDGMENTS

I am indebted to brothers and sisters and extended family members Asta, Emily, Ruth, and the late Harold Beck. Bev and Roe, Joyce and Wally, Dick and Joanne, and friends in Parkland have always "been there." The generous sabbatical leave policy of PLU has enriched my learning especially in global contexts; faculty colleagues Ralph, Bob, Audrey, Dwight, and Doug together with the Robert A. L. Mortvedt Library staff offered research assistance.

I acknowledge survey respondents, NAMI family members, plus social work and health professionals who have done much to keep me going. J. Dale Howard, M.D., has given extraordinary help.

It is difficult to thank enough the members of my immediate family, Bruce and Pauline, Ben, Ellen, and Anna. Without them, I could not have envisioned the work. John, of course, remains an unusual mentor.

Those acquainted with my wife, Alice, will recognize the one to whom I am most in debt; her unfailing sense of realities in our family's story provides a foundation for endurance.

Pacific Lutheran University
Easter 1994

PART ONE
Finding Out

1
Rage in the
Rec Room

Do not go gentle into that good night.
Rage, rage against the dying of the light.
　　　　　　　　　—Dylan Thomas (1914–1953)[1]

Jay's psychiatrist and I had a long talk about my son's future. For years each of us had tried in different ways to help Jay turn his life around. Today was different. For the first time the grim word "schizophrenia" entered the conversation. No change for the better was likely, I told myself. I hesitated by the office door. Turning, I asked, "What you see is what you get, is that it? How long will this go on?"

The doctor put his hand on my shoulder. Then I understood that endurance of long-term, challenging mental illness would be a part of our family's history.

The Story Begins

Bible reading comes alive when you eavesdrop. Everywhere, it seems, voices call out and hearers reply. Storytellers give snatches of intense exchanges:

> Isaac said to his father Abraham, "Father!" And he said, "Here I am my son." He said, "The fire and the wood are here, but where is the lamb for a burnt offering?" Abraham said, "God himself will provide the lamb for a burnt offering, my son." So the two of them walked on together. (Gen. 22:7–8)

But Moses said to God, "Who am I that I should go to Pharaoh, and bring the Israelites out of Egypt?" He said, "I will be with you." (Ex. 3:11–12)

"Simon, Simon, listen! Satan has demanded to sift all of you like wheat, but I have prayed for you that your own faith may not fail. . . ." And he said to him, "Lord, I am ready to go with you to prison and to death!" Jesus said, "I tell you, Peter, the cock will not crow this day, until you have denied three times that you know me." (Luke 22:31–34)

Later on, when the disciples of the Lord were threatened with murder, their major opponent traveled north from Jerusalem to search out more of them.

Now as he was going along and approaching Damascus, suddenly a light from heaven flashed around him. He fell to the ground and heard a voice saying to him, "Saul, Saul, why do you persecute me?" He asked, "Who are you, Lord?" The reply came, "I am Jesus, whom you are persecuting. But get up and enter the city, and you will be told what you are to do." (Acts 9:3–6)

The brief give-and-take conversations of the stories shape character, setting, and plot. What will happen next? Have Abraham, Moses, Peter, and Saul fully grasped what they have heard? Dialogue is common in biblical narratives. Those familiar with them will remember outcomes of power and promise arising as a consequence.

By Jay's last couple of years in high school, he and I had long since lost the capacity for dialogue. I began to slide on the slope of despair; he, in turn, seemed ever more moody and bad-tempered. Possibly he had good reason, since he seemed to have had his share of tough luck. At age sixteen, Jay's escape, with scrapes and bruises, from a motorcycle mishap became the prelude to an even more serious accident a few months afterward. While he was riding in the front seat of a friend's car, a collision sent his head crashing into the windshield. With hospital care and treatment from a plastic surgeon, apparently only a nasty nose and eyebrow scar marked the misfortune. (Given what I know now, a brain scan would have been in order.) But by this time there could be no doubt who the testy and grouchy member of our family circle was. His irritability grew into rebellion. He scorned, for example, family discipline involving "coming home at a decent hour." Still, for most parents of adolescents, was this anything new?

At first we took it for teenage behavior—stretching it, to be sure—marking the limits of a normal maturing process: He would "grow out of it." But it didn't happen that way; things only got worse.

When Jay was seventeen years old, something unusual happened. With our three children, my wife and I had taken a vacation from a sabbatical at London University and were touring Europe in our Volkswagen camper. We were in Córdoba, Spain, strolling one of its medieval streets. Jay was on the opposite side of the street, shouting and cursing. To this day, I have no idea what triggered such behavior. He always had a temper, but this was something else, scatological language released in a torrent of fury.

With considerable cajoling from home, he graduated from high school. He recorded scant employment success in the following year.

At last it was time to try college—away from home in the Midwest—for a fresh start. Making new friends might help. A suspension for use of a controlled substance, however, marked the fall semester. On top of this, a short time later an emergency phone call dashed our hopes even further: A third and more serious accident had happened. Jay was a passenger in a car involved in an accident in which the driver was killed. Jay flew out the door, and aid-givers found him in the ditch attempting to bury marijuana. The surgeon who patched him up assured me he was all right. But "there was something strange," he continued, "the language I heard from him when he came out of the anesthesia—awful. . . . I've never heard anything like it. Thought you should know."

Home again, bad temper moved from language to conduct. Once, for instance, on not getting his way, he slammed the thermostat with his fist and kicked in the wall underneath it. Then there was the time he yanked out the wires from an extension telephone. I had seen him groom his hair with such fervor that teeth from the comb began falling into the sink. When his brother, Brad, declined a challenge to fight (with no provocation whatsoever), he smashed his fist through a glass window.

Then came a new low. We were finishing breakfast one day when, once more, I declared use of the car out of bounds. This step had been taken because previously he had taken the keys and driven off even as I was running out, waving and shouting, to stop him. Now, suddenly, the table rose before us. Splashing juice, spilled milk, and clattering dishes fell into our laps with a crash. He had turned the tables, all right; with an obscene gesture and a string of obscenities, Jay bolted out the front door. Was this, I wondered, what psychologists meant by "acting out"?

As were Jay's maternal and paternal grandfathers and great-grandfathers, I am a Lutheran clergyman. We are church people; it is fair to describe us as pietists (no cursing allowed), but hardly as puritans in the popular sense. The tirade in Córdoba and the breakfast incident were so senseless, something unexpected and bizarre. It took years to accept powerlessness in the face of such behavior.

Months later, late one night our teenager burst into another rage at some minor behavior boundary line. This time he slammed the door of the downstairs rec room and turned up the stereo rock music full blast. Moments later I heard it—his voice, fearsome gibberish, shouting and babbling above it all! "Out of control," I decided, "and it doesn't belong in this house." I reached for the phone.

Five sheriff's deputies responded to restrain and drag our son and brother from his home. At least the awful rec room sounds had cleared from the air. We all needed sleep. Rage, it seemed, had finally reaped its reward.

Little did I realize then what would sink in later. Had such behavior actually signaled madness? Were such tantrums and defiance sinister portents of a bizarre transformation in the youngster we thought we loved and knew? Had they surfaced *apart from his control?* How often have parents disturbed by the behavior of a teenager thought of such a thing as this?

> The first psychotic symptoms of schizophrenia are often seen in the teens or twenties in men or early thirties in women. Less obvious symptoms, such as social isolation or withdrawal or *unusual speech,* thinking, or behavior may precede and/or follow the psychotic symptoms.[2]

A father's guilt and a son's paranoia would haunt the actors in that scene for years. Yet in retrospect, from that episode in the basement we had begun to climb our Mount Moriah and confront not only fear and desperation but also reality. Like Abraham and Isaac, we "walked on together" in grim determination. "Stumbled along" might better have depicted our gait. Years would pass as our journey unfolded, but, in the course of time, we too would reconcile at a place of sacrifice (Genesis 22).

Households on Trial

Calling the police meant I had finally turned away from expecting a solution through prayer. Reason also gave way. Had my survey of successful counseling methods—plus the well-planned assistance of professional counselor friends—resulted in progress? Definitely not, for the angry rebellion—combined by now with alcohol abuse—had only accelerated. Contrary to the notion that parents need simply recognize and correct a seeming overreaction like this,[3] deep inside I suspected there was more to it than all the ugliness leading up to that desperate telephone call. I felt more in tune with another father who had been having trouble with his son (Mark 9:14–29). When Jesus asked him how long the difficulty had persisted, his reply indicated it had gone on for years, ever since childhood; in this case, epilepsy apparently accounted for the symptoms of their struggle and chaos. Also despondent, he pleads for help, and at the Teacher's call for faith, cries out, "I believe; help my unbelief!" (v. 24). It was a final surrender; he had come to the end of his resources. Had I not also, that night? Even to the point of giving up on a youth in desperate need of help?

A "family disturbance" jail booking—help *my* unbelief! We had never dreamed of such a thing for one of our own, to say nothing of the "psycho" ward commitment to come. Had we failed that badly as parents? Biblical direction is forthright:

> Children, obey your parents in the Lord for this is right. "Honor your father and mother." . . . And, fathers, do not provoke your children to anger, but bring them up in the discipline and instruction of the Lord. (Eph. 6:1–4)

I remembered with new interest the words "I the Lord your God am a jealous God, punishing children for the iniquity of parents, to the third and fourth generation of those who reject me" (Deut. 5:9). Iniquities? We were, after all, praying, Bible-reading people. Had we taken for granted—too easily, apparently—our abilities to accomplish a biblical standard for family discipline, given that a leader of the church must "manage his own household well, keeping his children submissive and respectful in every way—for if someone does not know how to manage his own household, how can he take care of God's church?" (1 Tim. 3:4–5).

We were not alone in our bewilderment. Another parent sought

7

answers during the confused context of self-doubt and guilt when mental illness ultimately came to light in a child:

> What did we do to create this situation? Were we too lenient and lacking in discipline? Were we too strict? Did we love our children enough? Did we hold on too tightly and identify ourselves with them? Is there a better hospital, a better doctor, a better treatment?[4]

With medical cure still so elusive—at least by comparison, for example, to organ transplants—it has been easy to blame drug abuse and permissive families for adolescent crises ending in jail and psychiatric treatment. Here were chickens coming home to roost. Yet today psychiatry is moving from the study of the "troubled mind" to consider the "broken brain." Currently an explosion of knowledge about how the brain works has taught us that many forms of mental illness are due to abnormalities in brain structure or chemistry. Despite the continuing outdated misinformation placing the blame on dysfunctional and inadequate parenting, this reminder still comes as profound relief.[5]

What about the burden of isolation felt in families with a loved one who never seems to respond positively, no matter what? The experience of mental illness in our family has left me a bit skeptical of quick and decisive intervention strategies. In the wake of confusion mixed up with false hopes and fruitless leads, we have had to put on hold any doctrine of progress. We are skeptical but not without hope: The word "endurance" comes to mind.

Martin Luther had his share of troubles; as well as theological battles, there were struggles with illness, particularly in later life. He suffered from headaches, dizziness, family bereavement, a leg ulcer, and kidney stones; some investigators have even added mental illness to the list. His angry, vulgar language—combined with bouts of sixteenth-century "melancholy"—appear to them as indications of a manic-depressive psychosis.[6]

To the reformer, illness meant times of trials and tests. Eventually they became a part of his vocational consciousness. If the Christian life were *without* trials, he insisted, it could not ultimately become a life of faith; *conflict* comes with faith, and trials "keep faith in motion."[7] Luther's boldness came across again as I encountered its New Testament support:

My brothers and sisters, whenever you face trials of any kind, consider it nothing but joy, because you know that the testing of your faith produces endurance; and let endurance have its full effect, so that you may be mature and complete, lacking in nothing. (James 1:2–4)

In this you rejoice, even if now for a little while you have had to suffer various trials, so that the genuineness of your faith—being more precious than gold that, though perishable, is tested by fire— may be found to result in praise and glory and honor when Jesus Christ is revealed. (1 Peter 1:6–7)

Faith in Motion

Luther's own faith struggles moved him toward the "message about the cross" (1 Cor. 1:18). "I did not learn my theology all at once," he claimed. "I had to search deeper for it. . . . A theologian is born by living, nay dying . . . not by thinking, reading, or speculating." Theology must be attached to personal events and historical change. A "theology of the cross" discovers the presence of God not in manifestations of power and glory (a "theology of glory") but rather in the midst of peril, uncertainty, and suffering. It is a way into the darkness that must become the known context in one's search for light.[8] As one whose questions far outweighed his answers at the time, my faith moved in a flux of depression, but I had rediscovered a theological giant and mentor.

To stand by a person during the onset and treatment of an illness in his or her brain means (once the shock wears off) deciding never to say die. One abandons habits of crisis reaction in view of the long run. One finds oneself adapting, living *through* it but also *in* it. Strangely, one begins to live inside illness: thinking about it and discussing these matters at every opportunity. Some, like me, even write about it to bear witness to its dynamics.

Being ill is just another way of living, asserts Arthur Frank. Diagnosed at a relatively young age for both heart disease and cancer, he testifies about his illness, he explains,

[in order to] work out some terms in which it can be accepted. I want to enter into the experience of illness and witness to its possibilities, but not so far as to become attached to being ill. Seizing the opportunity means experiencing it fully, then letting go and moving on.[9]

Through his reflections on the crisis of disease and illness, Frank has succeeded in reducing my own fears about heart disease and cancer. I seek to follow Frank's lead in the case of mental illness.

The task is formidable. We are raised in a society that not only emphasizes self-sufficiency and high individual achievement but also stigmatizes those who ask for help with their episodes of unsettled thoughts and feelings. The stigmatized diseases of the brain are the last to be recognized and treated. A study of the public perception of disability groups has revealed a scale of acceptability. Most acceptable are individuals with obvious physical disabilities (using wheelchairs, for example). Then come sensory impairments involving sight and hearing. Developmentally disabled people and alcoholics are listed next. Those with mental illness are the least accepted.[10]

Through witness and education, I hope the mental illness category will move up the scale. Like Frank, therefore, I seek to draw on firsthand experience; yet not satisfied with this alone—and in order to avoid preoccupation with my own misery—I will also try to blend my anecdotes with stories from others. I seek to persuade readers that the most painful and humiliating experiences in life need not destroy anyone. Suffering is neither punishment nor something ennobling; it can, however, open possibilities for engaging a biblical theology of the cross and it invites us to clothe ourselves with compassion (Col. 3:12). This, I argue, is a good thing.

I will also attempt to shape a spiritual—mostly biblical—framework for thinking about the experience of mental illness. Since Luther's time, various approaches to Bible study have appeared. Analyses of its literary and historical background often concentrate on the origins of a biblical book. Besides a search for "types" (Adam and Christ) to enhance understanding, the hidden meaning of allegory (Noah's ark and Baptism) clarifies meaning. More recently, "contextual interpretation"—that is, interpretation from the situation in which either the reader or writer begins (liberationist and feminist, for instance)—has become apparent.[11] The latter method describes my biblical study: I examine texts from a "person with a disability and engaged with mental illness" context.

"We must wait for the text," writes a leading scholar, "that it may yield its claims at its own pace, only on its own terms."[12] Let me cite two passages that seemingly had waited to reveal their call in our growing family struggles.

Jay would come to be diagnosed for serious mental illness. For Jay's younger brother and sister, Cain's answer to the Lord concerning Abel, "Am I my brother's keeper?" (Gen. 4:9), yields a special claim today. Moreover, as an engaged parent, I look at Jesus' parable of the future great judgment (Matt. 25:31–46) with new respect for one of its visions. After the king identifies himself with the stranger, the naked, the sick, and the imprisoned, he compliments the righteous for doing the same: "Truly, I tell you, just as you did it to one of the least of these who are members of my family, you did it to me" (v. 40). For me, "the least" are now those struggling with delusion and hallucination, the least tolerated, the least understood, and the least served group in our society.

No single reading exhausts the potential connections of a given text with human life. From other biblical witnesses I will undoubtedly come upon unsuspected parallels. Together with other members of families like mine, I shall wait. Through our prayers, barriers of shame and isolation will continue to fall because others will see we have known the Lord's "steadfast love" (Ps. 36:5) and the "sharing of his sufferings" (Phil. 3:10). Our rage at the dying of sanity's light will have been shared and overcome.

2
A Domestic Chernobyl

I'm not only a father, I'm also a professor of psychology. . . . But, until my son was diagnosed (schizophrenia) at the age of 19, I had no idea what it was like to be a family member—living 24 hours a day with a loved one going through the agony of psychosis.

—Dale L. Johnson, Past President (1991),
National Alliance for the Mentally Ill

In April 1986 an inexperienced and tired operator at the Chernobyl nuclear power station in the Ukraine moved the control rods of Reactor No. 4 just slightly below the correct position. This seemingly minor oversight not only proved lethal to himself and others nearby but also created a giant plume of radioactive aerosol in the atmosphere. Within a few days the dangerous vapor had reached nearly every country in Europe and threatened to cast its fearsome shadow overseas. Thus occurred the most frightening catastrophe of modern industrial history, what has been called the most expensive accident in human history.[1]

Fallout from the mishap was recorded throughout Europe. Radioactive dust contaminated milk and reindeer. Back in Chernobyl it forced mass evacuations from a zone surrounding the plant. In addition to this threat to people and livestock, high above—roaming wherever the winds seemed to blow it—lurked an invincible cloud of radiation. The outcome seemed like a sentence of judgment respecting neither national power nor administrative boundaries. Would rain wash the deadly material down to earth once more? Recriminations of blame and fear of dangers unknown shook the lives of those who gradually conceded the menace and its potential.[2]

By a strange coincidence, the apocalyptic event in 1986 near Kiev has a counterpart in the New Testament apocalypse, the book of Revelation. Its foretaste comes from the plagues of Egypt (Exodus 7:8–11:10) in which one natural catastrophe—such as flies, boils, and darkness—succeeds another. In Revelation 8 the seer's vision of angels and trumpets announces disasters of hail, fire, and blood. When the third angel blew his trumpet, "a great star fell from heaven, blazing like a torch, and it fell on a third of the rivers and on the springs of water. The name of the star is Wormwood. A third of the waters became wormwood, and many died from the water, because it was made bitter" (Rev. 8:10–11).

The small, shrublike plant in Palestine called wormwood has a bitter taste, and its name acts as a biblical metaphor of bitterness and sorrow (Prov. 5:4; Amos 5:7). The prophet Jeremiah announces God's punishment in terms of wormwood and people having to drink of its biting and poisonous waters.[3]

Chernobyl means "wormwood" in Ukrainian. Rather than assert that the nuclear accident was a fulfillment of biblical prophecy (as some have done), I will focus on its legacy of mystery and plaguelike effects. In the domestic Chernobyl issuing from the haywire perceptions triggered in a diseased brain, every family member sips from a bitter brew.

Psychosis Fallout

Little by little I conceded failure to gauge, much less control, the poison our home atmosphere took on after the rec room incident. My cloudy memory today covers a seventy-two-hour weekend commitment in the psychiatric ward of downtown St. Luke's Hospital, during which I was let into a locked facility for a visit with my son.

A respite of several weeks provided even grounds for cautious optimism that our family had at last turned a corner on all this. But gradually the radiations of Jay's sullen demeanor and late hours out with unknown friends spread unspoken fears. Often he did not return by the next morning, and soon he moved into a house occupied by several other youths we had never met. Together we transferred some modest personal belongings and furniture and promised to keep in touch. For one whose knowledge of psychiatric terms at the time was street lingo (a neurotic builds castles in the sky; a psychotic lives in them), I would soon learn more: A neurosis meant a milder disorder such as anxiety or depression; more severe was a psychosis involving mania or schizophrenia, which often became incapacitating. Even at this early stage I sensed the second of the two diagnoses was the more plausible.[4]

The shadow of catastrophe would only spread. The guilt and shame I felt on entering St. Luke's locked doors to visit a family member on the psychiatric patient floor grew into awe at the nightmare visits now beckoning at Fir Lane State Hospital. Our Jay "was hyperactive, confused and delusional with visions of God talking to him," according to the report of the examining physician there. The youth also "entertained suicidal thoughts and had been urged by a friend to enter Fir Lane for help." Furthermore, the record continues, "Since fifteen he has used marijuana, angel dust, and LSD . . . and has had bouts of psychotic decompensation."

For some time I had suspected drugs as part of our mix-ups at home. Sure enough, Jay now began to tell someone other than his friends about it. It was worse than I had imagined. The full extent of my foreboding was borne out when I came across expert information disclosing how drug abuse and psychiatric disorders may interact and aggravate each other in an escalating cycle:

> Alcohol and other drugs are repeatedly used to relieve boredom or counteract feelings of rage or despair until they seem necessary for ordinary functioning. In a pattern typical of addictive behavior, the drug dependence results in actions that cause guilt, shame, and humiliation, and the alcoholic or addict takes dubious comfort in further drug abuse.[5]

Moreover, patients who on release from the hospital abuse alcohol and illicit drugs seem to be making an attempt to relieve the side effects of medications prescribed for treating their underlying disturbance. Symptoms are diverse and difficult to nail down for treatment; as a result, things often go from bad to worse, and the caregiving process must lengthen.

Jay remained at Fir Lane for an evaluation period extending beyond his previous seventy-two-hour involuntary commitment at St. Luke's. The first state hospital log entry ends with a reference to home and family: "Parents are described as devoted, seemingly unable to effect change." The estimate was certainly correct at the time, and no word like "seemingly" was necessary. Already the impact from what would be diagnosed in this onset state of affairs as manic depressive psychosis had outdone all of my ideas for turning things around.

Drifting Miseries

Self-deception and fantasy also enter the dynamics of shouldering the burdens of confusion and anxiety. It happens when things calm down, medical and counseling interventions appear effective, and this time, for sure, light seems to shine through at the end of the tunnel. "I was in a state of denial during the first stages of Niel's illness," a parent named Joy acknowledges. It would take years before she became wise to the fact of her son's schizophrenia, and even then she did not comprehend what it would require of her.[6]

The pain of psychotic illness retreats in some households by the apparently self-limited span of the acute stage when the turmoil settles after a few weeks or months. For other families the first hospitalization traumas are only the beginning of a long and arduous journey. They are forced to recognize the truth of chronicity; their loved one is released and improved, but still showing, once in a while, the symptoms pointing toward crises yet to be faced. They sense, at last, the truth that fluctuating, gravely disabling conditions will be the lot over the years ahead. At this point, however, our family mostly wallowed in ignorance, isolation, and apprehension.[7]

For years Grace and Jim Anthony readjusted their expectations as parents of Roger. At the same time they reflected about their apparent mistakes; often they wondered what it means to be "good" parents.

"We live from day to day," remarks Grace, "and you have to shed dreams in the face of undreamed-of realities." Self-blame and guilt feelings hurt the most. In reading all she could get her hands on about family issues, she encountered an idea made famous by Frieda Fromm-Reichmann in 1948. Rejected today, it contends that an essential failure in the maternal response of the "schizophrenogenic mother" produces schizophrenia. Further, Grace read about the "double-bind" theory Gregory Bateson advanced in 1956. In this thesis not only the mother's parenting is deficient but also the father's. Somehow the communication between the two of them contains so many mixed messages that as a result the child is overwhelmed in an intolerable double bind. And speaking of binds: What parent could ever come to terms with the notion of having *driven one's child insane?*

Like so many others, ourselves included, perhaps such notions contributed to their feeling like casualties of the indifference and suspicion they encountered from certain mental health professionals. When she eventually rejected this cup of remorse, Grace spoke up for scapegoats across the country: "We tried. We were conscientious parents—not perfect ones. And we had a child whose needs had been hard to meet. Not only by us but by his schools and teachers and now by other institutions." [8]

Marybelle Walsh has collected the confessions of other wounded family members:

I don't know how my other children feel about it.
We can't talk without crying.
We don't get together at family get-togethers.
My husband had to be treated for depression.
We are prisoners in our own house.
I aged double time in the last seven years.
It's as though he has a terminal illness, except he never dies.
It is our biggest problem . . . to look at this handsome, intelligent, formerly kind and good person and see him suffering so much.
Our costs were $40,000. Might as well have flushed it down the drain for all the good it did. [9]

Before these troubles began at our home, I had played the by-stander role as far as any serious contacts with mental illness were concerned. By this time, however, I was becoming more aware and also finding out more. Having grown up with *Life* magazine photos of asylum horrors, I never challenged the reasonableness of cause theories like the double bind and faulty maternal care. Thus the liberation I felt from reading E. Fuller Torrey's information was as exciting to me as if an authentic lost letter of Paul had just been verified: "There is no evidence whatsoever that schizophrenia is caused by how people have been treated either as children or as adults; it is a biological disease of the brain, unrelated to interpersonal events of childhood or adulthood." [10]

Moreover, as in a practical internship learning situation, I not only had second thoughts about the Hitchcock film *Psycho* but also was discovering personal resources in the crucible of exposure to real-life symptoms.

Sometimes people react to emergencies as if the right response had already been rehearsed. It was like that once when, shortly after a hospital release, I spied something peculiar in the kitchen: the tablet containers. As I recall, there were the four of them—newly prescribed—all lined up neatly in a row on the dining room pass-through shelf. They were empty.

Jay, I discovered, was already drowsy in the rec room easy chair downstairs, but there was no panic.

"Okay," I said, "we're going downtown." Dreamlike, he heard and obeyed.

The emergency room nurse scanned the container labels and my intoxicated companion. There were no questions or forms to bother with this time. White-coated personnel appeared and took over. I wondered if the stomach-pump treatment had saved his life, but no one ever mentioned it later on. One of the longer hospitalizations followed.

Occurrences like this one took their toll on our family and professional lives. Weariness joined anxiety and sadness. Would there ever be a respite from it all? Would we ever see our way through?

Babel and Babble

Being a parent in such a state of affairs presents a challenge to communication similar to those symbolized by the destruction of the tower of Babel: a confusion of tongues about directions for care and healing. But to have first heard the babble of a manic episode hit hardest; it was dramatic, awesome, and even frightening. When the uproar arises in one's own child, add heartbreak to the spectacle.

Soaring towers in the skylines of cities from Sydney to Seattle frequently catch the tourist's eye. Ancient Shinar, in the Bible land of Babylon, also boasted a spire, the tower of Babel (Gen. 11:1–9). As is the case with the Genesis stories of the Garden of Eden and the Flood, Babel's eventual ruin also portrays God's judgment on the continuing sin of humanity. As a consequence, the Lord "confused [in Hebrew, *balal*] the language of all the earth; and from there the Lord scattered them abroad" (v. 9). Babel and confusion weave a play on

17

words. "Babble City" and its lonely, vacated tower are signs of disorder and communication breakdown.

A telling insight near the end of the story reveals the Lord's plan to confuse the language of its builders "so they will not understand one another's speech" (Gen. 11:7). But the Hebrew text further allows the translation "would not" hear, they "would not" listen to one another.[11] Later God would establish the norm for his people as an "ear" community: "Hear, O Israel: The Lord is our God, the Lord alone" (Deut. 6:4). Then the communication perspective sharpens: "Keep these words. . . . Recite them to your children and talk about them" (vv. 6–7). Parents are to listen to the commandments and promises of God; they, in turn, must nurture their children to hear and act on them as well. Police intervention in the rec room seems to have signaled the raw demise of the "ear community" at our house. Debate and conflict had taken its place. What had gone wrong? Why do children refuse to listen? Why do they disobey parents? Why must it come to jail bookings and psychiatric wards?

"Train children in the right way, and when old they will not stray" (Prov. 22:6). I thought as parents we had complied—with due warnings about drugs, alcohol, and smoking—and glibly assumed successful communication. If "old" can mean maturity at age twenty-one, however, our son had "strayed" plenty already. Why this rebellion to the point of self-destruction? Yet not only did the question of why stymie us, but so did the questions of what and how. What was really happening—drug abuse, turbulent adolescence, family dynamics, a combination, or something else? How should we respond—tough it out, learn better methods of discipline, seek help (if so, from whom?), or bargain around the household for relief?

In the drug-available culture of the mid-1970s, a child in another family chain-smoked cigarettes and had easy access to the marijuana he used so obsessively. So his parents began to suspect, as we did, that more was involved underneath it all. Was the drug use, they asked themselves, an unconscious attempt at self-medication to prevent those unpredictable outbursts of rage? Then, too, such abuse might have hastened the onset of mental illness itself. Whatever the facts, Neil's behavior became increasingly disturbing: "He would rush into the house and jump into a bathtub of cold water, believing that was the only thing that would save him from dying," his mother remembered.

18

Further, she recalled, "One Christmas Eve I stayed up all night in a freezing house—he'd turned off the furnace because he thought it was spewing poisonous gas into the air." [12]

Many parents brood for months about powerlessness in running up against the effects of their offspring's drug abuse. Sam's mother remembered how he "started off so well"—with his own paper route at age nine. Seven years later he lost a factory job for lying on the floor and going to sleep. (In our case Jay had gotten along well as a restaurant waiter, but his next job as a shoe salesman ended when he argued with customers and spat on the floor.) After three years in a mental hospital, Sam returned home. His mother still questions if all that medication was good for her son.[13] So do I.

Gladys Mittleman's experience of crisis paralleled mine. After days of vacillation she decided the tensions around the house had become unbearable and were threatening to get out of hand. She called the police. They soon arrived—lights flashing—as neighbors watched and wondered. Law enforcement officers themselves know that a "family disturbance" is unpredictable, and intervention can even be fatal. But what Gladys remembered most was the humiliation of it all; later she thought of others like herself who, trapped in much the same dilemma, delayed the decision to seek help and waited for years before getting an ill relative out of the house and into hospital care.[14]

Trial and error, revised opinions, failure, and humiliation—I learned the hard way. An uncompromising instructor, brain disease, presented a syllabus including police intervention at home, symptoms of schizophrenia, and reality-based knowledge of the insane asylum. By now, our family was broken or "dysfunctional" and needing outside help. We needed to graduate with credentials of survival and hope. Until we made the grade, however, I would study any means of holding on within my family and through the mental health system. Leaning on other class members having firsthand experience, we had rehabilitation as our term paper topic. And most of us would gain our degrees.

I have attempted to chart the conflict in figure 1. Starting from ignorance and misinformation, child and parent respond to symptoms of communication breakdowns in ever-widening circles of failure. Social intervention resources in the community then become necessary to build toward a more effective response.

SYMPTOMS   RESPONSES

Child	Parent	Early Level	Eventual Outcome
"Discipline problem"	Confusion and anger	More discipline attempted	Child defies and parent despairs
Dropout siblings school friends	Blaming Poor school Alcohol Street drugs "Growing up" phase	Desperate measures Alternative settings: school, retreat center	Disappointment False hopes Letdown Worry affecting others, job Consideration of outside intervention
Delusions and/or hallucinations	Bewildered	Anxiety Fear Denial "Learned our lesson" Hope	Worry affecting family life Loss of control Admission of Failure Shame Guilt

IGNORANCE AND MISINFORMATION

FIG. 1. PARENT AND CHILD: CHARTING THE CONFLICT

Babel from Inside

What is the view from the other side? How does the person in the center of the hubbub fare in the turmoil? What does it feel like to leave home this way? One of them writes, "In our prime we were stricken by something that had no name. . . . It shattered our lives. It was a thief who robbed us of our dreams, our plans, our future." Then came the hospital ward:

At that moment when we most needed to be close to the ones we loved, we were taken away to a far off place. . . . We were told we were mentally ill. At the age of 14 to 17 or 22 we were told that we had an illness with no cure. We were told to take medications that made us slur and drool, that robbed our bodies of energy. . . .

We were told to share our secrets. We were told that, in time, we could go home.[15]

One representative of those who work with and plan services for individuals with mental illness suggests that too little attention has been given to reading the private musings of persons in their care. For her, their thoughts even appear poetic and artistic. "Robert," for instance, longs for recovery:

> Fill my mind with knowledge
> Fill my body with definition
> Fill my life with total well being
> Fill my pockets with money
> Fill my head with normal thoughts
> Fill my nerves with relaxation
> Fill myself with the old me.

A patient at the same hospital who signed her name as "Hilda" nourishes hope. She asserts,

> I've got room for friends
> I've got room for sunshine
> I've got room for laughter
> I've got room for fortune
> I've got room for tomorrow.[16]

Others, recovered from their ordeal, disclose both insight and burdens. "Ed" asks,

Do you know the hurt I feel when I look into my family's face and see their fear? Fear of me and what I have become. I try to tell them I will not hurt them. I try to explain it is not their fault. I try to reach out to them . . . I cannot hide the agony of my own soul.[17]

In the same vein, "Esso" links courage and hope to overcoming. She "tells it like it is":

We are met by profound silence by all when we ask if we will ever be all right. Imagine our feelings of worthlessness as we are continually bounced from hospital to hospital, transferred from doctor to doctor, switched from one medication to another. . . . Feel our shame . . . and anger—as we realize that life will not be as we had planned, and please know our extreme difficulty in finding hope and courage to overcome this constant fear and ongoing sense of failure.[18]

Meanwhile, back at the house, anxious parents, having been "unable to effect change" themselves, had never dreamed their futures would come to this. Marriages break up on these rocky shoals, for sometimes people just throw up their hands and leave. Still, others refuse to surrender and keep trying to effect—somehow, some way—a means to overcome.

At this point I made a decision similar to one taken by a father whose son involved their family with the issue of homosexuality: "When I found out, I soon decided I had to either stand with my son or support the rejecting attitudes of society. I chose to stand with my child."[19]

So would I, in the face of the unknowns of serious mental illness, back my son. He had already led his parents into a new land, one we never would have chosen to visit. But when we stopped for a look around, we were relieved to discover that other pioneers, sisters and brothers of an extended family, had already joined the tour. We would hear the stories of their offspring, listen for advice, and search out a new language of witnessing.

3
Of Cuckoos Nests
and Loony Bins

He lived among the tombs; and no one could restrain him any
more, even with a chain; for he had often been restrained with
shackles and chains, but the chains he wrenched apart, and the
shackles he broke in pieces; and no one had the strength to subdue
him.

—Mark 5:3–4

Sharing the pain evolved from bitter frustration. Providing shelter,
giving advice, and flexing discipline boundaries would also merge
into a support role. I drove a private taxi to the doctor, brought cigarettes, and often coordinated access to the various social service agencies. In addition, there was the parental open line of credit. Other
specifics of caring—answering the midnight telephone call and visiting the hospital room—framed a video of stress.

Family Asylum

Another DWI. By now Jay had made the acronym familiar: driving
while intoxicated. Yet this time was different because the social
worker informed me Jay was in jail.

"He's in the tank," Mike, the social worker, announced on the telephone.

"The tank? What's that?" I asked.

"Well, it's a place where they sort of hold all people together—
you know—who are awaiting hearings and so forth." (As a matter of
fact, I did not know at the time, and what a decisive event it would
turn out to be.)

I hesitated. "I see."

"But listen," Mike went on, "he's doing okay. I've checked on him, so don't worry, I'll get back to you." He was downright cheerful. But I never heard from Mike again.

Two days or so passed, and this time Jay was on the line. Desperately, he pleaded, "Dad, that new leather sport coat I got? Sell it for bail money!" That was all he could say.

I knew about the sport coat all right, because I had covered the check he had written to pay for it. (Eventually I learned how phone calls from the tank were rationed, timed, and sometimes fought for.) Still, this time I was determined: Having gotten himself into this mess he would have to see his own way through the consequences. Enough was enough.

News of the hospitalization came from a source I cannot now recall. Police had found their charge, naked, with his head in a toilet bowl, and they committed our son to Mercy, the nearest downtown hospital.

A turning point—Jay was never the same again.

The psych ward of Mercy Hospital provided sanctuary, and I was thankful. After all, *jails* are for custody and punishment, not treatment and care, are they not?

Days afterward, a judge, an attorney, and several social workers and medical people convened for a formal judicial hearing in the ward to determine if Jay was capable of understanding his situation. Further, they sought to evaluate his need for continued treatment. An attorney, I learned, always represented the patient's rights in the face of involuntary commitment procedures. (I was politely admitted to the hearing but ignored thereafter.) Jay himself—eyes partly closed, head bobbing slowly, and half stupefied from his medications—sat at the head of the table. He seemed to preside over the macabre drama where his fate hung in the balance.

Some time later, stabilized and released, he returned home. Plans for finding work or getting on with college studies went on indefinite hold. Rather than try to plan or predict the next move, we simply depended on medications and hoped for a change. It came, but not in the way we anticipated. I experienced a new facet of hospitalization several weeks later.

Discovery of the limits of state hospital admission policy and my own ignorance came the day Jay was waiting for me when I got home from work. He had previously been treated at Fir Lane State Hospital, but I was amazed to hear him murmur, "I want to go back to Fir Lane." In minutes we were on our way. It was dark when we came through the gate. The high ceiling of the turn-of-the-century room with its tired fluorescent light bulb added shadows to our gloom.

Clipboard in hand, a short man—with white coat just like in the movies—appeared. Jay began to pace.

"Name and address?" he asked, and scribbled away. "I'll see what I can do."

"What do you mean?" I countered. I thought Jay had taken a remarkably constructive step forward and could not imagine that anyone here would think otherwise.

"We cannot admit just anyone off the street." He spoke in a soft voice, and I detected an African accent. When I disclosed how much Ann and I had appreciated sabbatical teaching in Tanzania, he spoke of his home in Nigeria.

Jay stopped pacing and glowered.

The thought of bringing him back to the house—with all that night-time pacing—was unbearable. "But my son is ill. He has a file. He's been in here before!" I thundered.

The small, sad face said nothing.

"I am a citizen of this state and I *demand* this man be admitted."

Another long pause. "Come with me, young man." Homeward through the dark rain I savored my ridiculous bluff. No "snake pit" here for our family—it provided both haven and respite. At least my Nigerian sympathizer could chalk up an interview with a "disturbed American parent." Yet, just months ago, how could I ever have dreamed of gratitude for the favor of placing one of my family members in a mental institution?

Perhaps in that incident Jay and I had stumbled across an earlier version of Western culture's insane asylum as a temporary necessity, brought on by emotional trials, providing shelter along a path to recovery. Before further scrutiny, however, let me investigate biblical connections.

Asylum in the Bible

At the time of Israel's entry into the Promised Land, six of her Levitical cities were designated as places of asylum, havens of safety or protection from enemies where someone who had accidently caused a death might seek refuge from avengers until his case was decided by the elders of the city. Furthermore, if he were found innocent of deliberate murder, he could continue to live, protected, in the city of refuge.[1] The story of Lot in Genesis also suggests a background of hospitality extended to those in need of shelter and comfort (19:1–29). Yet this was not always the case either.

Consider David's flight from King Saul. He had sought hospitality from another monarch he feared, Achish of Gath. Measuring David's strange behavior (feigning mental illness), the ruler turned to his servants and asked, "Do I lack madmen, that you have brought this fellow to play the madman in my presence? Shall this fellow come into my house?" (1 Sam. 21:15).

Long ago another family was trying to cope with symptoms of a serious mental illness in a loved one. "Then he [Jesus] went home; and the crowd came together again, so that they could not even eat. When his family heard it, they went out to restrain him, for people were saying, 'He has gone out of his mind.'" (Mark 3:19–21). Sensational healings of the sick, exorcisms, and a confrontational teaching style had gotten out of hand. Furthermore, when rumors began to circulate in public that Jesus had lost his senses, it was too much; his relatives went out to take him back into their custody at home. Today they might have called a community mental health center for assistance from a mental health professional to help determine if the young man was a "danger to himself or others."[2]

Suffering patients sometimes defeated the best efforts of families and others in Bible times too. Recall the "Gerasene demoniac" in Mark. The full narrative here (5:1–20) suggests that the symptoms of illness were both violent and persistent; efforts of family and others in the community to restrain the person so obviously a "danger to himself or others" had failed. This ended with the pathetic victim's social isolation out on the mountains among the tombs, a first-century snake pit scene. This unfortunate man, the shame of Gerasa, thus had nothing to qualify him for mercy save the horror of his standard of living. Then Jesus intervened, not with simple kindness but rather with another of his "deeds of power" and proffered wondrous rehabilitation (Mark 5:6–20; 6:2).

Long before that family trouble in Nazareth, officials in the highest circles of government in Israel had attempted to take charge of King

Saul through a diagnosis and treatment plan for what we might today call music therapy for clinical depression.[3]

> Now the spirit of the Lord departed from Saul, and an evil spirit from the Lord tormented him. And Saul's servants said to him, "See now, an evil spirit from God is tormenting you. Let our Lord now command the servants who attend you to look for someone who is skillful in playing the lyre; and when the evil spirit from God is upon you, he will play it, and you will feel better." . . . And whenever the evil spirit from God came upon Saul, David took the lyre and played it with his hand, and Saul would be relieved and feel better, and the evil spirit would depart from him. (1 Sam. 16:14–16, 23)

Saul's evil spirit responded to David's lyre by taking leave, and the future king's reputation advanced. Musical magic, however, was hardly available for us at Fir Lane. I felt more in tune with other biblical voices like the wandering Abram: "As the sun was going down, a deep sleep fell upon Abram, and a deep and terrifying darkness descended upon him" (Gen. 15:12).

I began to discover a kinship with the elder David at prayer:

> Save me, O God,
>   for the waters have come up to my neck.
> I sink in deep mire,
>   where there is no foothold;
> I have come into deep waters,
>   and the flood sweeps over me.
> I am weary with my crying;
>   my throat is parched.
> My eyes grow dim
>   with waiting for my God.
>
> (Ps. 69:1–3)

Calling on Jay behind a hospital's locked door provoked mixed feelings. He was safe, and at least we knew where he was. The sinister-sounding telephone calls (drug deals?) tapered off at home, and we fit more easily into daily work routines. Yet the defeat and failure represented by his confinement goaded fantasies of a new treatment setting that would work; perhaps another counselor or different medications would supply the magic answer. For now, however, the psych ward management by chemistry took priority. Jay would need to be "stabilized" first. Hearing "protective crisis intervention" language only shielded the reality of a desperate perplexity.

Asylum U.S.A.

Can you think of a surer conversation stopper than "she had to see a shrink" or "he wound up in the mental hospital"? I recall someone contorting his face and doing a little jig on mention of the "psych ward." This is unfair, to some extent, and mental hospitals have gotten a bad press for decades in this country.

Growing up in the United States during the 1940s, I had little accurate knowledge about the insane asylums I heard mentioned from time to time. My impressions were formed mostly by Mary Jane Ward's grim 1946 book *The Snake Pit*. Two years later a movie based on the novel, starring Olivia de Havilland, reinforced the horror and shame of it all, and likely planted a few seeds for current conversation stoppers.

The popular magazine *Life* came out with a 1948 article going even further: Institutions for the mentally ill resembled Nazi concentration camps like Belsen and Buchenwald. In awful echoes of the Holocaust, it revealed that patients had been beaten to death in them. In addition, startling photographs lingered in the mind of anyone willing to look long enough. One was captioned, "These Byberry [Philadelphia State Hospital] male patients are left to live day after day sitting naked on refuse-covered floors without exercise or diversion."[4]

Now in its sixty-eighth printing and with seven million copies in circulation, Ken Kesey's novel *One Flew over the Cuckoo's Nest* continued the verbal assault of the 1940s into the 1960s and 1970s. The hero, McMurphy, is placed in a mental ward and suffers the oppression of an institution typified by Big Nurse Ratched and electroshock therapy. He will discover how the system of care is actually indifferent to his wishes and welfare. A 1975 film version directed by Milos Forman and starring Jack Nicholson continues to reinforce this contention for millions of citizens. Changing from con man to hero to savior, McMurphy descends to lobotomy surgery and sacrifices his life. This inspires his counterpart, Chief Bromden, to arise in dignity and freedom. Thus a message of *Cuckoo's Nest* is that "something can be done about absurdity."[5] I wonder.

For the 1990s Kate Millett's *The Loony Bin Trip* maintains the "patient versus the System" literary genre. In it she portrays her incarceration in an Irish hospital. Forced medication, isolation, and brutality result in a devastating loss of confidence and self-esteem. She questions if mental disorder should be treated as an illness at all.[6]

Criticism of the state mental hospital took on a new dimension with the appearance of Erving Goffman's book *Asylums* in 1961. To write it, the author spent a year doing field work within St. Elizabeth's Hospital in Washington, D.C. (which had seven thousand patients at the time), perfecting a technique of participant-observer research. Taken as a whole, he concluded, the institution became a dehumanizing, demoralizing, and humiliating additional burden on the patient. Through his scholarly technique using empirical evidence, "the mental facility care system's cover was blown once and for all." It was difficult, claims one authority, for them to pretend any longer to be anything other than warehouses for "society's unwanted human refuse."[7]

In ancient Israel the sins of the people were symbolically placed upon the scapegoat, which was driven into the wilderness, out to the demonic figure of Azazel (meaning something like an "angry God") as a final answer to family and community failures (Lev. 16:8, 10, 26).[8] Today the scapegoating of mental hospitals continues.

As a "parent consumer" I shall not try to deny the accusations. Still, I suspect the issue is more complicated. Such a major unaddressed social problem needs scrutiny from another angle: What is the alternative? How can human dignity in these circumstances be protected and enhanced at the same time? Which mistakes of the system need correction first? Could public education relieve the stress and promote a more humane version of the admirable aspects of ancient and medieval hospitality?

At both Fir Lane and Mercy hospitals, I found fairly pleasant inpatient quarters. A corps of aides, nurses, and others stayed with patients around the clock to provide food, comfort, and security. Sessions of talk therapy, combined with medications prescribed by a supervising physician, rounded out the treatment plan. Calm when I came to visit, Jay's appearance in general verified the benefits of his newfound refuge and shelter from what I could only imagine had taken place in that jailhouse tank.

Because I had expected to see some psych ward white coats of medical authority, the casual civilian dress everywhere surprised me.

The women who unlocked the door and sat behind the central desk I surmised must have been nurses who supervised medication schedules. Who were the others? Aides? Social workers? Maybe even a psychiatrist or psychologist? How could I tell the difference between another parent, a chaplain, or even another patient? There were no introductions, informational pamphlets, or hints of treatment modes. And Jay remained mostly silent.

In this lonely family crisis time, I was nonetheless grateful that at least someone else had acted on Jay's need for medical care instead of additional jail time. Soon, I told myself, we would stop running in circles; there were be a new start with this nightmare fading to oblivion. After all, Jay had not actually been "sent away" to any cuckoo's nest loony bin; he had gained access to a time-out period when he needed it most. Release for "rehabilitation in the community" was soon to be at hand.

Community, to my chagrin, was never clearly defined; moreover, eventually I would find out about treatment floundering in separation from recovery planning. It was like driving without brakes or flying without wings. I would have to wait and hold on.

PART TWO
Holding On

4

Faith and Frenzy

Caregivers are confronted not with an ordered sequence of illness experiences, but with a stew of panic, uncertainty, fear, denial, and disorientation. The caregiver's art is finding a way to allow the ill person to express his needs. Eventually a balance must be worked out between what the ill person needs and what the caregivers are able to provide.

—Arthur Frank

"Illness," writes Arthur Frank, "gives us permission to slow down." It teaches us the value of being alive. As far as our children are concerned, he asserts, we see them only in relation to what they will do when they become adults. Yet children can also become critically ill. Frank acknowledges how painful it is to remain open to such an experience. It reminds us as parents that our assumption that we will not have to see our children die is an illusion.[1] For me, at least, so is the notion that children are immune from insanity. This has been brought to light in our family and in many others as well.

"Insanity" is a legal term used to cover the degree of accountability one may or may not have for criminal acts (the insanity defense). Prior to what was happening in our family, I had not connected the word with sickness or illness. The same was true with "madness": it usually conjured up visions of insane asylum horrors.

I have since learned to set aside the stigma-laden terms "insanity" and "madness" in favor of the words "disease" and "illness" in attempting to tell the story of what happened in Jay's life. "Disease," a medical word, has to do with measurements of the body and studies of "dis-ease" occurrences within it. Illness takes on the process of living in or through disease. It begins where disease leaves off.[2]

33

In this chapter I touch upon drug therapy (regarding disease) but pay more attention to the illness side. Hence, I will earmark day-to-day happenings involving mental illness around the house and at the same time track down elusive spiritual insights both unsettling and comforting. Daily anxieties gave way eventually to healing and confidence that I would become a parent who would live with mental illness in an adult child without becoming a victim of the toll it took in my life.

Everything Lost but the Struggle?

Authorities report that at any given time between thirty million and forty-five million Americans—nearly one in five—suffer from a diagnosable mental disorder involving a degree of incapacity that interferes with employment, attendance at school, or other activities of daily life. The personal costs from untreated mental disorders are similar to those for heart disease and cancer. The Institute of Medicine estimates the direct costs at 23.4 billion dollars a year. Moreover, suicide is the fifth leading cause of death among people between the ages of twenty-five and forty-four, and the third leading cause of death among children.[3]

The term "schizophrenia" describes a puzzling situation, with multiple causes and disorders; it affects approximately one percent of the population. It creates psychotic (out of touch with reality) episodes that may occur only once to some people; others, however, may undergo many incidents during a lifetime. During the interim they can lead relatively normal lives. Schizophrenia often affects the five senses. Persons suffering from the disease sometimes hear nonexistent sounds, voices, or music or see nonexistent images. Because their perceptions do not fit reality, they react inappropriately to the world. Yet it most often develops gradually, and close friends or family might not notice the changes in personality as the illness takes initial hold.[4]

Let me shift from "disease" language to the "illness" context, with a few anecdotes mostly about the months and years of "initial hold" at our house.

All at once Jay jumped up from the table, sped off, and slammed the front door behind him. "It's another one of those door-slamming parties, I guess," sighed his sister, Erin. Cake, candles, and presents were highlighting the birthday celebration (hers) at our house.

Outside, just as he had behaved at other family get-togethers, Jay sat on the lawn puffing furiously on a cigarette and by now utterly distracted from anything inside. Before long, crumpled stubs would jam an ashtray he took along. This time we sensed his presence through the wall: urgent, high-pitched, strange subvocal sounds. At times what sounded like a dog's muffled bark broke through the stormy monologue.

Ann reacted first and spoke for the rest of us around the table. "Has Jay taken his meds today?" she asked quietly. It was rhetorical; we already understood: from all indications, probably not. Yet who could tell? Because everybody—ourselves and other caregivers at that time—wanted Jay to become as independent as possible, who would vote to start intervening again with that question? Yet once more we felt tempted because things went so much better when he took his prescribed medications faithfully. Conversation around the table trailed off and we sat listening and appalled. (The new neighbors across the street—what ever would they think?) I told myself that the unsettling behavior was a temporary setback. He had snapped out of it before. Likely he had heard those voices again—too removed for our perception—issuing shattering insults, threats, and commands. Solitude with nicotine, I decided, had built a first line of defense against them. Yet I well remembered similar disturbances over the years.

We moved along the freeway, Jay and I, in no special hurry. Traffic was light, the sun was out, and I could not fault my partner's driving. He had stabilized really well, I thought; it was gratifying to see him engaged in a simple pleasure. There were, after all, not too many left after his recent hospitalization.

For no reason we moved into the right lane and, to my surprise, pulled over to a gentle stop on the shoulder.

"Dad, you can drive."

"But Jay," I said, "why? You're doing fine."

"No, it's okay," and by this time he had skipped out the door. We changed seats.

He was quiet on the journey back, but I'd grown used to that. To-

35

day I surmise the voices he heard out on the freeway were hardly quiet, and that their dire commands gave him only one alternative: pull over and stop.

More than a dozen years have passed since then, and during them Jay has never so much as hinted he would want to take the wheel again, hardly typical for him and most other youthful Americans.

Things were all right at the start of our errand when we entered freeway traffic. Abruptly, however, Jay left my side to lie down on the van bed. Grunts and groans, tossing and turning—through the rearview mirror I saw him tearing at his hair. "If I had a gun, I'd kill myself!" he screamed. Then "Stop!" The truck weighing station came up just at the right time, and when I had pulled over the grimacing youth burst out the side door to commence a rapid, circular, jerky pace.

For the first time, I saw tears on his face. To want to help and yet to remain helpless—is there worse anguish for a parent or spouse?

On a longer venture our destination was a state park about an hour's drive distant. Ann and I thought we'd invite him along because he had been so "good" lately—calm although perhaps unusually quiet.

Things were going well, I thought. If Jay did not wish to enter the conversation, what did it matter? But just as we rolled to a stop to pay the entrance fee, the silence broke. "Let me out," he commanded. Puffing a cigarette, he walked furiously to the edge of the plaza in the direction of the woods. From the corner of my eye I spotted the check-station ranger reaching for a walkie-talkie. I intercepted him just in time.

"It's okay, he's our son." Puzzled, he laid aside the device and stared. Sure enough, moments later our passenger—on the same fast beeline—popped into the car once more as if nothing had happened. He banged the door closed, and we were on our way again.

As we would discover in the months ahead, as a religious family we were not alone in our struggle with perhaps the most chronic and disabling of the major mental illnesses. Consider the case of another sufferer.

For years a young woman, Sylvia Frumkin, had been in and out of schools, hospitals, and other living arrangements while struggling with mental illness. Her condition steadily deteriorated, and finding the appropriate combination of medications puzzled many physicians.

The Klopfer family, devout Christians, offered to let Sylvia live with them. Providing a job (teaching art to their daughters) in exchange for board and room, they also agreed to give Sylvia doses of megavitamins.

The Klopfers believed Sylvia was possessed by demons. When she mumbled a lot George Klopfer intoned, "Sylvia, I come against these forces that are making you mumble, in the name of Jesus, and I demand that you stop mumbling."

Sometimes it worked. But some days Sylvia would not clean her room or get out of bed. Klopfer would cry out: "There is power in the blood of the lamb . . . and I demand that you dress yourself now."

Sylvia would not budge. The hosts felt themselves losing the struggle. With signs of health problems of their own coming on as a consequence, they called the Frumkins to admit their best efforts had failed.[5]

Is biblical faith an achievement of the will? If so, together with the Klopfers and others, I had not successfully qualified as compared to other Gospel examples I will cite later. For my part I would hope in the *gift* of faith and assign the full measure of its visible evidence to God and the future (see Eph. 2:8–10).

No Balm in Gilead?

Six centuries before Christ three questions framed the lament of a prophet in Judah.

> Is there no balm in Gilead?
> Is there no physician there?
> Why then has the health of my poor people
> not been restored?

> (Jer. 8:22)

On the one hand, to the first query the answer could only be yes; Gilead, after all, was famous in Israel for its healing ointments. The second question also called for an affirmative reply. Many physicians would be in the area to prescribe the various medicines. On the other hand, no answer to the third was in sight. Apparently those in Jeremiah's audience had refused to listen or repent. As a result, an inward spiritual hardness had prevented genuine reform, and the political scene approached chaos.[6]

Is there balm for mental illness? For me over the past few years the word "crazy" had taken on meanings beyond absurdity and silliness. I had seen chaotic, senseless craziness come and go without warning. It ranged from sudden door-slamming agitation to months of stark and sober-faced apathy. Social withdrawal inevitably followed but not so far as to prevent bursts of incoherent thinking and bizarre statements. "I am quick," Jay would announce on occasion. And, "Don't you *know* I'm Stevie Wonder?" (It became an inside family joke to relieve tension when Brad sometimes applied the moniker "Stevie" to his brother.) Jay would compliment his sister, Erin, "You are conscientiously comprehensibly astute."

For a long time I suspected that street drugs and alcohol were keeping this turmoil alive. It was for that reason, I concluded, that over a period of two years the jobs begun with high hopes always ended with dismissal. Jay spent one semester at a local college, but he shunned those who reached out and kept to his room; later I learned he had pounded the walls with his fists. Incomplete grades closed this door of opportunity.

A radical effort to counter such habits involved a plan for joining an out-of-state drug rehabilitation program. Having agreed to a pledge of good intention and discipline, Jay paid the price of a radically short haircut and headed south. Could it be true? Were we past the roughest spots on the way to restoration? The answer came a few days later when Brad appeared at my office to announce, "Dad, Jay's back. He hitchhiked." In my frustration I recalled the comment of a counselor as to how resourceful he thought Jay was whenever the need arose: always quite "verbal" (manic?) and so forth.

What now? The cycle of promise and setback had brought us back to the square marked "Go." "We know," asserts Paul, "that all things work together for good for those who love God, who are called according to his purpose" (Rom. 8:28). When it comes to the things about serious mental illness, the promise becomes difficult to sustain.

One time Jesus spoke of faith to a woman who had come for help: "Daughter, *your faith* has made you well; go in peace, and be healed of your disease" (Mark 5:34; italics added).

When two blind men approached Jesus for recovery of their sight, once more the potent faith factor came into play. The Lord touched their eyes and said: "According to *your faith*, let it be done to you. And their eyes were opened" (Matt. 9:29; italics added).

Is faith something you have only as an individual or is it also something one shares, as when reciting the Apostles' Creed with others? One finds both aspects in the Bible. The woman in Mark 5 sought Jesus out; so did the blind men of Matthew 9 who followed him, begging for mercy. These anecdotes have a personal, emotional framework and illustrate "having faith." Acknowledging their trust, Jesus responds with healing. Why not also today?

In the prophetic questions cited, Jeremiah makes an implicit promise: Return to the divine Torah, and blessings will replace a seemingly hopeless institutional turmoil in Judah.

Intellectually I had answers for such questions, but emotionally the fears I felt in trying to cope with schizophrenia's wake threatened the faith I was working with, made me doubt that I would ever have *my* eyes opened, be healed, or go in peace. For me, trusting in our family's Gilead physicians—hospital personnel, friends, counselors, drug prescriptions—began to replace the loosening spiritual moorings. Only when I received the gift of a sense of my total *powerlessness* to change things for the better did I begin to note at the same time God's Gilead balm. I would let Jay be responsible for taking his daily medication and look no further ahead than to that day's reward of peace.

A Disease like Any Other

Like magic, the words kindled hope: lithium and antidepressants. Each of them, in addition to neuroleptics and others, identify antipsychotic medication therapy. Soon, around the house, we could recite the exotic trade names scribbled on Jay's prescription slips. As heralds of treatment and stability, they eventually created a fanciful creed of salvation lighting a way through the mysterious medical attention we had begun to depend on.

Henri Laborit, a French surgeon, observed how medications related to promazine, which was given prior to operations to prevent surgical shock (a serious drop in blood pressure), accounted for a surprising side effect. Both before and after surgery, patients appeared less anxious, almost tranquil, about their trauma. Even while their calm lingered, they nevertheless remained aware of activities around them. In addition, they could still communicate. The physician pondered: Would such a medication prove useful in psychiatry? Thus, in 1952, the first step of a modern biological revolution took place.

The following year an American, Nathan S. Kline, working in a New York State laboratory, set out to isolate the active ingredient of serpent-wood (*Rauwolfia serpentina*), a root used in ancient Indian Vedic medicine to calm people. The researcher published his findings in 1954, and as a result the chemical reserpine, one of the first tranquilizers, appeared on the medical scene.[7] At last, medical science had powerful new weapons for counterattacking the baffling origins and ravages of madness.

A small paperback supplied a breakthrough in my quest for more information. Its author, a psychiatrist, even shared my theological concerns:

> You may have a religious background or be a religious person . . . I, too, am a religious person and I believe that religion can often illuminate or help relieve psychiatric problems. . . . And I hope that after reading this book you will no longer feel shame, fear, or guilt; that you will become a crusader for a future age when mental illness is recognized as what it is—a disease like any other.[8]

She then cited the large amount of evidence suggesting that mental illness is caused by biochemical abnormalities and structural brain abnormalities; weakness of will, bad parenting, and bad marriages are not to blame.[9] This helped me appreciate the effects of medication as a scientific therapy (even with its trial-and-error efforts) to calm Jay's emotions and settle his angry behavior.

Researchers today anticipate development of new drugs to treat more than two million Americans with schizophrenia. Older antipsychotic drugs like haloperidol—after forty years still the most widely prescribed schizophrenia treatment in the world—relieve typical symptoms like delusions and hearing voices in about 70 percent of patients. But they are less helpful in dealing with secondary symptoms like withdrawal, lack of energy and motivation, and an inability to experience pleasure, the symptoms already only too familiar in our family.[10]

Other investigators are also taking up the challenge. A recent *Harvard Mental Health Letter* reports:

> Brain imaging will be refined to provide further knowledge of changes in brain structure and functioning. New substances will be found to trace neurotransmitter pathways. Genetic linkages will be uncovered as the human genome is thoroughly explored. Discoveries about the structure of nerve receptors will aid the search for better drugs, which in turn will make other forms of therapy and rehabilitation more effective.[11]

The medical and research focus is fascinating but has a tendency to distance people from the human side of things. Mental disorder increasingly prompts scientists to search out facts with a view to curing symptoms, yet publicity of the quest will not prevent ongoing stereotyping of the insane and glib mockery of those "crazies and weirdos out there." The struggle at our house touched more than simply a "young adult male hearing voices and withdrawing from social contact"; it was embodied in our son and brother. And because I had by this time been thwarted so often, run so many errands, and paid so many bills on his behalf, I also began to share his trials. Mental illness had come to stay at our house.

5
Give Us This Day
Our Daily Meds

Our Father in heaven, hallowed be your name. . . .
Give us this day our daily bread.

—Matthew 6:9, 11

Anxiety does not empty tomorrow of its sorrow—
only today of its strength.

—Charles H. Spurgeon[1]

Today's trouble is enough for today.

—Matthew 6:34

In my art of caregiving I had learned to rely upon Jay's daily medications to deal with his symptoms. Taken faithfully and according to the directions, the treatment at least gave him a respite from the frenzy that turned into punched holes in dormitory room walls. Even so, I grew restless during the passing months; I could not seem to avoid looking back with regret and ahead with fear. Jay was "gravely disabled" (in social work language), and I could see why.

Yet, "faith," as I recalled from another biblical text, can also embrace "an assurance of things hoped for" (Heb. 11:1). From within, however, I stubbornly refused to surrender faith in my own ability to do something about the matter. Bringing theology further into the picture, I pondered God's ability in place of mine, and the divine capacity to "accomplish abundantly far more than all we can ask or imagine" (Eph. 3:20). So how about a young man like Jay having the ability to leave home, compete, and become independent as his former Boy Scout chums were doing? And how about an ability to contribute to someone or something?

Mental illness, in fact, continued to disable both father and son at the time. What was there to hope for beyond "control therapy"? Must the faith of a Christian with a disability differ from that of more able-bodied Christians who seem to get their prayers answered?[2] We avoided hospital wards and trouble on most days during times of stabilization (medical language), but we still had far to go before achieving either social or spiritual "maintenance." Meanwhile, my vision of future rehabilitation and healing would remain on hold.

Trails and Trials

Karen Lebacqz has described the dilemma of parents of a newborn infant afflicted with atrophy of intestinal tissue as a "wilderness experience." Several elements are involved: (1) disruption of normalcy (they are at the hospital day and night); (2) recurring uncertainty (one day things look good, the next day is a crisis); (3) loss of control (the medical world takes over); and (4) loss of identity (life no longer matters). The experience of such a crisis, the author suggests, bears similarities to the wandering of the ancient Israelite people.[3]

In Bible study, important words are often overlooked. At first glance, "desert" refers simply to geographical location. Yet it also puts students on the track of historical event, narrative, and religious insight. The desert recalled for Israel its sojourn in Egypt and the exodus drama. Christians remember John the Baptist's desert appearance, as well as their Lord's temptation in its solitude. The biblical word for desert also signifies a territory that is desolate or beyond, that is, outside the limits of governmental control and consequently disorderly or dangerous.

In the Bible, desert, above all else, looms as a place where faith is tested. The children of Israel traced wandering paths in the desolate Sinai desert, all the while tested to determine whether they could live in complete dependence on God apart from the accustomed security of Egypt.[4] God would lead both his people and his Son along desert trails where each met "the world" in its essential state. The threat of devil and demon in its midst was not a cause to flee but rather a time for trust in covenant promise. In the most challenging locale of all, they could manifest God's rights and victory.[5] Through trust in divine promise and submission to God's will, the desert also became a territory of expectation and pilgrimage. To demonize desert wilderness limits its realities because faith and hope can also spring forth from the challenges of its trails.

Although travelers in the outback prepare themselves for safari

43

rigors, they often find themselves surviving on the margin of things. Ordinary routines become a thing of the past when daily needs must be met. When we lost control of the trails we had to follow within the mental health system, I sensed Sinai in the offing. At this point, seasoned by disruption of normalcy and loss of control, our family continued to navigate through thickets of therapy.

Hitting Bottom

Eight years lapsed from the time it all seemed to start back in Córdoba until a psychiatrist gave the enemy its name: affective schizophrenia. Without clinical details, here is a list of people and places I encountered during the wilderness trek:

People

three psychologists
four psychiatrists
two attorneys
two clergypersons
three mental health professionals
two social workers
twelve (or so) high school teachers, college professors, and
    friends

Places

three colleges
one private psychiatric hospital
one state mental hospital
two public hospital psychiatric wards
two courtrooms
one jail
two halfway houses
two hospital emergency rooms
one shelter for the homeless
one drug rehabilitation center
two church outdoor ministry camps
one congregation

The pattern hardly matches the prevalent dreams of middle-class parents for their offspring: high school, college, graduate school, marriage, and a profession that affords upward mobility. Each person and place on my list represents a different lead, a new effort, and an attempt to start over. Behind it all was our effort to understand what was taking place. One day it was abnormal teenage rebellion; the next it was drug abuse or family dynamics or stress.

Of all the persons involved, the psychiatric profession seemed both to hurt and to help the most. Consider these examples:

When I learned the identity of the doctor who was treating our son, I pleaded for an appointment to talk about the situation. We spoke several times on the phone. No, a conference was not possible. I would have to be satisfied with a voice on the phone. An announcement was the final word: "If your son doesn't stop using drugs, he will destroy himself." (As if I did not already know!)

We discussed our family history and the prospects for our son at an exclusive and expensive psychiatric hospital. The physician dismissed us with these words: "Your son has a mental disorder— whatever *that* is." Another psychiatrist asked, "Why do you bring this situation to me? [Implication: Can't you see how busy I am?] You will have to tighten up at home." We were wondering at the time if kicking holes in the wall, ripping telephones from their sockets, and smashing the thermostat—all before our eyes as we attempted to "set parameters"—were not unusual teenage behaviors. (Imagine the irony—years later—when we listened to the same medical authority inform an audience that recent theory shifts blame away from family dynamics to biological causes of the illness.)

Seeking information at a public hospital psychiatric ward, I implored one of the attendants (in civilian dress) about assistance from a "mental health professional" who, as I understood, was available through a local community health center. I sought advice: Could I help in a treatment plan? Should I avoid contact instead? The only response was a contemptuous stare. How could I have known at that time that *I was talking to* one of these mental health professionals?

"He has to hit bottom," announced the counselor. It was the end of my quest for a new start or answer—anything. "I know it must not be easy," he went on, "but back off. He's got to want to *help himself.*"

Jay would have to learn that behavioral choices have consequences for which the instigator has responsibility. In turn, his parents should recognize their enabling role; getting him through just one more scrape actually protected him from having to face the outcomes of bad choices. Growing up was postponed, and for Jay's own good it was time to back off.

This counsel was reasonable and, I believed, offered in good faith. Suddenly I had a flashback: "Come now," cried the prophet, "let us argue it out, says the Lord; though your sins are like scarlet they shall be like snow" (Isa. 1:18). Sins (destructive behavior) are assumed, but the promise of *forgiveness* outweighs both argument and failure. Religious reality's balance of caregiving clings to daily repentance and the fresh start.

Jay should not have been the only sinner subject of the consultation. Had not our counselors avoided or denied the likelihood of an illness severe enough to rob a person of reason? Had not his parents surrendered to professional expertise and ignored resources within their own family's religious faith? Looking back, I am inclined to answer yes.

At that time, however, we decided on tightened discipline to promote change. If our son would not come home at a reasonable hour, he was no longer welcome. We would keep the doors locked at night. Yet in the cold darkness, to keep the door closed before the solitary, unshaven, and disheveled figure standing in the porch light meant anguish difficult to describe. It went against what I think must be one of the deepest instincts of any parent. To have provision and power but refuse it to your own child is a fierce test of endurance. How often Ann and I *almost* opened that front door.

He slept in the lawn equipment shed a few nights and then asked a favor: Could he hitch a ride downtown? Nearing our destination, he asked to stop for a "treat." Sure: pie and coffee at a dimly lit restaurant counter. Afterward no words were exchanged as he picked up his meager belongings and headed out into the night. On his own, he would have to find a "mission" or church-run shelter. Alcoholics and addicts would be roommates; bright college kids were now a curious thing of the past.

On the way back toward our warm and comfortable suburban home, the splashing of windshield wipers kept time with the flooding waves of my sadness. Even if someone had thought to ask how Jay was doing, what would I have said?

There was no contact of any sort for nearly three weeks. Early one morning as I grasped the door handle of our aging Volkswagen van, a movement startled me. The bed was down, and, to my immense relief, Jay appeared.

"Let's talk about things" was all he had to say. We headed for breakfast. Bottom had been reached.

Jordan's Banks

With the best intentions and goodwill, most of the other people and places involved also tried to help, but, in the final analysis, they proved as impotent as I was to cure or rehabilitate. Eight years it took to find out—eight years of false hopes, confusion, guilt feelings, and helplessness.

For me learning the eventual truth—finding out—was the key to holding on. Light began to overcome the dark side of my parenthood dreams, and I discovered life after mental illness. Words like "stabilization" and "maintenance" became terms of confidence. Contact with other parents in the same situation was water in the desert. Volunteer work at the local mental health center became therapy. Fortunately, self-pity is the earliest casualty in contacts like these.

"I think I can help Jay," Doctor H. stated. For some years this doctor has accepted state medical coupons for a modest fee. Among the several psychiatrists we consulted, he was the one finally to venture Jay's diagnosis. Gradually, through psychotherapy and medication, this therapist enabled a stabilization and maintenance period with rare crises. For the first time in years of uncertainty, we found someone to lean on.

It is not my intention to minimize the difficulties faced by mental health professionals in advancing therapy strategies and procedures. Diagnoses are multiple and often baffling. In cases involving substance abuse, victims appeal to the system for rescue from the effects of illicit drugs on their minds, yet afterward they stoutly resist further rehabilitative measures. By such behavior, some circumnavigate the path to recovery and enter their own revolving door. When "the organ of decision (the brain) is also the organ of disease," however, we might expect as much.[6] Moreover, the case system remains overloaded by the demands made on it. Case workers, underpaid and held accountable for a whole list of persons behaving like Jay, become overwhelmed. (If the availability of weekend services is the gauge, mental illness apparently avoids those days.) The stress as I had observed it a few times was that of constantly trying to get out from under the casework load. Besides, they sometimes had to hold their breath for the next state or federal funding decision. Little wonder I felt at times like an unwelcome intruder when I approached one of their mental health center desks for *any* news—good or bad—of what was going on.

In the Old Testament book of Numbers, a theme is repeated that, in spite of the providence of Yahweh in the exodus wilderness wanderings, the people murmured complaints and even rebelled against their leader Moses. Yet the ancient tradition also affords insights of how the people were forged together into greater unity and solidarity through bitter struggles and suffering.[7] Something akin to this developed in our family odyssey.

In the New Testament, Paul learned to forget the ugliness of past struggles because he chose to press on to a distinctive new quality of life and a future prize (Phil. 3:13–14). I still need to let go as the apostle managed to do. I seek to break out from various feelings.

Anger

There is enough around for everybody. Insofar as Jay was responsible, I am outraged with him for throwing his life away. It hits me whenever he "comes back" for fifteen minutes, and I see once more what he had going for him. I rage at drugs in this country. The understaffed and bureaucratic system still irritates me. I am also fed up with the stigma of mental illness and the vicious stereotyping promoted by movies and television.

I am angry at myself for being duped by so many for so long.

I am disgusted that my church trumpets justice in distant lands and ignores Lazarus (Luke 16:19–31) on its doorstep. Had enough? So have I. I want to let go of all my anger, and the guilt besides.

Guilt

If only I had known about my local mental health center. Then I could have called there the night I phoned the police instead of watching those five sheriff's deputies drag Jay from his home. If only I had been a better parent. If only we had managed a brain examination (CAT scan) following that high school accident when Jay's head shattered the windshield of the car he occupied. If only I had not sinned. If only God had heard our prayers. (No—let it go, and press on.)

Ignorance

Today I employ acronyms like CCF (congregate care facility) and words such as "tardive dyskinesia" (involuntary face, tongue, or lip tremors, a side effect of medication) to explain Jay's occasional frowns. Ten years ago, I was more or less like everybody else when it came to knowledge of mental illness. I was one of "them," the ones bearing their backpacks of ignorance. Listen to them as they display some common prejudices and test their assumptions against reality.

Prejudice: Nervous breakdowns are a cop-out and a sign of a "weak personality."
Reality: Chemical imbalances of the brain produce symptoms of psychoses.

Prejudice: Mentally ill persons are dangerous.
Reality: The vast majority are passive and often prefer solitude.

Prejudice: It's up to the state to take care of *those people.*
Reality: Mental health professionals are eager for individual and group volunteer efforts from synagogues and churches.

Today, silent as Trappist monks, Jay and his board-and-care housemates sit before a humble meal. From such "least of these" (Matt. 25:45) and their eerie nobility, I have something yet to learn.

Suffering

Dietrich Bonhoeffer, Christian martyr of World War II, cautions the faithful from his Tegel prison cell:

These things must not be dramatized. I doubt very much whether I am "suffering" more than you or most people are suffering today.

Of course, a great deal here is horrible, but where isn't it? We so like to stress spiritual suffering, and yet that is just what Christ is supposed to have taken from us.[8]

This voice of another giant of theology reminds me to grasp the divine promise more firmly.

The best advice I got was from the father of a mentally ill daughter. "I spent thousands," he said, "before I decided to let the system take over. It works. Give it time." This man gave not only practical guidance; together with his wife, he also comforted us and became what I suspect the Bible means by a "helper" (1 Cor. 12:28, RSV). They helped us dismiss romantic visions of miracles, divine or medical. Grace has intervened. Both sets of parents are grateful that emergency room trips with our loved ones (on discovering slashed wrists and empty medication bottles) were made in time. Today Jay remains one of my closest friends. How many parents of "normal" children can say the same about their young adult offspring?

What does a parent dream about for a child? For the majority, I submit, it is not a place of renown in politics, entertainment, or sports. Rather, the dream concerns life in the long run. We hope for a child's happiness and that he or she somehow will help others along the way. Fame is fine, to be sure, but is it not more of a gift or a surprise than the result of a plan? The unexpressed dream, perhaps, is an ancient one: you plan to overcome mortality through your children.

Mental illness puts an abrupt end to this and sniffs out other dreams of how life was meant to be. The result is loss, not unlike bereavement. You wander in the wilderness and watch your child die in a socially unacceptable way. Early on, it was like putting funeral plans on hold. Yet eventually we lowered our expectations and managed to abandon a few of the cultural dictates of success. It was then that we caught our first glimpse of the banks of Jordan.

6
Exodus to
Main Street

In some instances families can sustain a relative's chronic demands only when the person does not live with them. One form of assistance that families need most is access to residential housing they can rely upon. Parents, children, spouses, and siblings actively join the social work staff in the search. Relatives are fully aware of what the mental health worker can only guess: living with that particular individual would drive others crazy.

—Phyllis Vine[1]

Before long, practical realities overtook my faith intangibles. Our family had already voted to identify with Jay and share his pain. Still, sleep-ins, his pacing at night, and the incessant smoking and coffee drinking (lots of sugar) of someone with time on his hands wore on the household routines. If Jay had another place, we concluded, our support could adapt to his routine there. The search was on. To begin with, the social work staff took charge, as they do to this day. Later we worked out apartment locales not far from home and in cooperation with them.

Toward the Interstate Viaduct Asylum

Yet living arrangements for Jay—set forth with such optimism—never seemed quite right. There was "The House," designed for helping clients push beyond their halfway situation. Halfway to where? "Independent" living, a job, and starting a new family? Such dreams were not on the map at the time. Foster home arrangements came next. They also failed, for various reasons. An apartment with a roommate lasted a bit longer, and a single-room apartment showed promise for more than a year. Yet Jay's total indifference to personal hygiene

51

and upkeep made the setup untenable. I disdained putting my signature to the statement of responsibility demanded by the landlord. Erin, Ann, and I, joined by friends with whom we had begun to share our plight, cleaned and repainted the unit. So what next? About half the time families become the primary caregivers.[2]

"The modern family," states a leading social critic, "is the product of egalitarian ideology, consumer capitalism, and therapeutic intervention." Moreover, efforts of the "helping professions," he maintains, "have subjected the relations between parents and children to the supervision of the state, as executed by the courts, the social work agencies, and the juvenile court."[3] In broad terms this may be true; I can only testify to the contrary in terms of my family. For us these professionals—psychiatrists, psychologists, and social workers—began to live up to the title "helping" in what we endured. Their counsel and assistance, however experimental and imperfect, furnished direction away from edges of despair; other families may have a different story, but for us their support saved the day. Later I learned how the difficulties we faced were part of a much larger picture.

"The care of the seriously mentally ill in twentieth century America has been a public disgrace," writes E. Fuller Torrey. "Over fifty years of warehousing patients in inhumane state hospitals has been followed by almost forty years of dumping them into bleak boarding homes or onto the streets." He concludes by contending that to dump some 400,000 seriously ill individuals into communities that neither wanted them nor had adequate housing for them will be remembered as the hallmark of deinstitutionalization. Another critic comments that the old stereotype of the drunk on skid row was being replaced by the reality of the schizophrenic on skid row: "from Thunderbird to Thorazine."[4]

How did this come about? In the early 1960s the success of new antipsychotic drug treatments had surprising results. President John F. Kennedy called for the establishment of community mental health centers across the land to replace reliance on mental hospitals. "Deinstitutionalization" had begun. Inclusion of the word "health" in the name of these new centers was supposed to diminish the negative public stereotyping suggested by its opposite (illness). Yet it did not work out that way; "health" came to support prevention services. No wonder: One looks for treatment success stories, and such are hard to find when it comes to the major disorders of depression and schizophrenia. Gradually, public education and the needs of the individuals seeking consultative services got most of the attention. The primary mission to treat serious mental disorders took second place or was forgotten. Kennedy had made no reference to counseling services for married couples who had difficulty communicating, young adults concerned about their relationship to the opposite sex, or middle-aged individuals undergoing existential crises. The President was proposing a program for the suffering sick, not the worried well.[5]

The situation therefore hides the plight of those people who suffer from chronic mental incapacities and need help the most. Denial of unsolvable problems seems to spawn freedom from responsibility for them. Who has ultimate accountability for providing adequate treatment in today's mental health care system? I wonder; people still fall through the cracks.

The unstable, oftentimes confused and frightened client, set free from the asylum or state hospital, was asked to relate to a wobbly, politicized, undependably staffed, and underfunded series of offices. There are the mental health centers (without hospital units), the bureaucratic social and health service locations (state and federal levels), the local food banks, the housing authorities, the rescue missions, and, usually at the bottom of the list—just before nights in the street or under a bridge viaduct—the church shelters (provided space is available). Maybe an all-night bus ride or a shabby eatery provides survival. It is enough to test the mettle of the sanest and healthiest individual around.

A "Danger to Oneself or Others"

Imagine a public response to heart disease treatment if it were delivered in the same way: First, a bureaucratic, red-tape cluster of national "cardiac health centers" requires those with this disease to present medical-legal just cause (difficult to obtain) for hospitalization if a "cardiac breakdown" occurs. Then, once patients are under treatment, doctors see them for perhaps fifteen minutes a month for medication at the center. It is up to clients to get there on their own, even if this means walking for miles. A cardiac episode requiring hospitalization specifies stabilization and discharge in five to ten days unless the patient is ruled a criminal (having somehow wound up in jail overnight along the way) or is admitted as an "involuntary commitment." Meanwhile, at the "state cardiac hospital" criminal patients are housed on the same grounds as everyone else. As for the hospital itself, perhaps an accreditation probationary status for understaffing or other conditions is in effect. How would Americans respond to such health care for heart disease? There would be a public outcry. Local and congressional investigations and media attention would boost a rocket of change. Funding would appear. Citizens across the land would not tolerate such a national disgrace.

Government judiciaries and mental health centers fail to provide an adequate alternative to hospitalization as envisioned in 1963. Too many of those eligible for "community-based care" continue to drift into the revolving-door syndrome: from psychiatric ward to an apartment to the street or shelter to a congregate care facility, back to the street or jail, then to the hospital once more. Here civil libertarians add fuel to the fire. In temporary hospital courtrooms, attorneys and judges plead, advise, and decree—and then wash their hands of it all, even when the proceedings take place in psychiatric wards in the presence of the nodding, stupefied, and tranquilized client, like Jay, about to be released. At least, libertarians reason, society has defended the individual's civil rights. Given the quality of the life these civil liberties afford on release, it is easy to conclude that ideology has replaced both compassion and common sense. On the western frontier, people died with their boots on. Today, people die "with their civil rights on."

Attorneys of the "mental health bar"—by concentrating exclusively on individual autonomy litigation—failed to recognize that a disease process had already curtailed the individual's liberty. Medical treatment often becomes the only avenue for restoring a person's autonomy in the first place, at least in any meaningful sense of the term. The common adjective "crazy" is there for a good reason; sometimes a person is really out of it. Still, this is no reason to refuse or abandon medical treatment. Secure in their antipsychiatry dogma that mental illness is a fiction or a result of mental institutions that actually make people sicker (à la *One Flew over the Cuckoo's Nest*), they committed patients to the streets. However, the mental health bar failed to put comparable efforts into lawsuits seeking to force establishment of community treatment programs.[6]

I advocate a change: Instead of the criterion "danger to oneself or others" for involuntary hospitalization, make it "unable to care for oneself." This is easy to demonstrate. Ask any sibling or parent. In case after case, the seventy-two hour involuntary commitment time is not sufficient for stabilization. Imagine an exhausted parent (the writer) coming for a hospital visit and being told his still-hallucinating son has been released ten minutes earlier to hitchhike home. Periodic legal review (thirty to ninety days) would control the "putting someone away" threat.

Eventually, the whole apparatus of public care drifts; responsibilities shared on different care levels become responsibilities denied on every level. Clients pay the price. Forgotten and lonely inmates of congregate care facilities (of nursing homes and of various "inns" and "lodges") who need wholesome companionship spend their days before the television or staring at the walls. And make no mistake: Facilities of this sort operate in industrial areas, in wasted central cities, or out in the countryside. Jay has lived in each type. Railroad tracks are more common in them than either parks or playgrounds, I have noticed. Only once was the living arrangement in a "respectable" neighborhood. Sure enough, after Jay had spent two weeks in a comfortable tract house, a neighbor approached me as I parked in its driveway: "Who *is* that guy in the back yard? I'm going to do something about it!" Jay moved once more a few days afterward. Social workers intervened ahead of me.

A recent government report asserts that about six hundred community mental health centers have received a total of several hundred million dollars in federal construction money in the past twenty-five years. In return they agreed to provide—for at least twenty years—basic services including emergency treatment, inpatient care for the severely ill, day treatment for those who could live at home but needed intensive care, outpatient services, and education services to schools, hospitals, and other institutions. The inspector general's report estimated that at the beginning of the 1990s some 250 of the 600 have failed to provide such services.[7]

Until one becomes system-wise, involvement with these mental health services (federal, state, county) is like dancing with an elephant. Parents, while waltzing to the music of evasion and confusion ("We don't handle that here"), see the body and spirit of a son or daughter crumble. Amid the chaos, family members lose their innocence about the suffering produced by these intractable, baffling disorders. Parents, spouses, and siblings are loaded with demands for rescue: Can you front me some money? Will I go to jail? Episodes of various degrees of seriousness generate an atmosphere of crisis and emergency.

When, through medicated and foggy eyes, Jay focused on the "home address" space on a form to request public assistance, what could he fill in? As a last resort, he would have to stay put with congregate care long-term intervention and simply continue from day to day.

A Clubhouse Called Home

His last jail episode and whatever else had happened during his life on the streets apparently lit a fuse within Jay: He would listen to and obey others apart from the ones pronouncing street corner rules of the game. For several years, including the months of his parents' absence during a sabbatical leave spent overseas, Jay made the most of our local Pacific Community Mental Health Center's (PCMHC) services, including a protective payee role for supervising spending of a monthly government Supplemental Security Income (SSI) check. Most of it went for board and room costs at Start Over House, a board and care operation supervised by PCMHC personnel.

Best of all was the center's Rose Club, an adult day-care facility designed to reflect the successful Fountain House, a New York City center for the psychiatrically disabled. The club has *members,* not patients. It functions as a social center instead of another treatment facility.[8] Operating from a building in a busy city industrial section (and close to a bus terminal), the Rose Club features a thrift shop and luncheon cafe on the first floor. A spacious supply room and a sitting area are adjacent. On the second floor are social worker offices and a classroom. Jay has worked in the kitchen and taken turns as the luncheonette cashier. Even though he has been unable to move out into the regular world of work, other members have done so.

For a time Jay (with close ties to PCMHC personnel) moved again into a suburban home with two other club members who tolerated his behavior: heavy smoking (outdoors or in his room), occasional vigorous pacing, plus gesturing and talking to himself, with what experts call "subvocal activity."

In addition, social workers took considerable efforts to assist Jay in becoming more independent. They taught him cooking skills, took

	Action	**Attitude**	**Prospect**
Son/Daughter	Medication Housing, social Club regulations	Survival Accommodation Discipline	Rehabilitation "Independence"
Parent	Provide support (outings, etc.) Stay in touch with care- service providers	Welcome, stranger! (Loved ones as they are *now*) Endurance	Make out will Hope
Care-service Provider	Maintain plan for individual, i.e., housing, physician Communicate change to parents	Patience in personal contacts Professional detachment as called for	Experiment with new strategies Keep up in academic field Vocational goals

FIG. 2. THE CHRONIC PLATEAU

him on grocery shopping tours, and arranged a shared-time use of kitchen facilities in the house he shared with others also risking greater freedom.

The venture was called off after several months. Jay was showing a precipitous weight loss and an even more blunted response to their efforts. Supervision, including meal preparation, seemed to be the answer for the time being. Eventually a long-term respite period emerged.

Looking back, we had worked through many complexities in diagnosing mental illness and its treatment in our nation's deinstitutionalization climate. The limits of our family resources also became evident; furthermore, we discovered how the investment of time and energy in trying to manage Jay's symptoms and provide some support took us from activities we neglected elsewhere. Caregiving exacts a price. Although not looking at our problems as insurmountable, we began to think ahead about making out our wills and how the conditions of a will might affect Jay in times to come. A chronic plateau table (figure 2) summarizes the environment.

Jay is there on many a page in old family photo albums. Today his sober countenance freezes any action I detect in pictures taken at family parties. As I turn back the leaves, nothing of this sort emerges from those schoolday vacation and Scout hike photos of a decade back. Shyness and hesitancy are hinted at, perhaps, but surely no suggestion of what he would someday become. No clue leaps out at me from those childhood and adolescent mementos as to how he would teach me the meaning of all I never wanted to know about schizophrenia. There is no hint he would eventually haunt a jail cell, psychiatric wards, and board-and-care dining tables or that he would learn to survive daily medications in order to subdue the frightful sights and sounds seizing his brain.

As he posed at a lake during vacation time with siblings and cousins—most of them now parents and successful in various professions—who would have guessed he was to play the odd man out with such terrifying vengeance? Who could have known he would never finish college? Who would have set odds against his ever holding down a job, marrying, having a family, or leading a life like these peers of his?

Our family will never be the same. Jay is still a part of us, all right, and we share the wounds his twilight world exacts. In the order of things, in living with schizophrenia, the pain—more or less—is inescapable. Yet so are understanding and love, so is a strange new joy of welcoming Jay in our midst for what he is *today,* and so also is a curious peace in accepting our pasts while at the same time being set free from them.

7
Care in Focus

But we were gentle among you, like a nurse tenderly caring for her own children.

—1 Thessalonians 2:7

Effective psychosocial treatment must often be sustained indefinitely, just as antipsychotic medication must be maintained indefinitely. Both must be provided on a long-term basis, indeed for a lifetime in many cases.

—*Resource Book for Psychiatric Rehabilitation: Elements of Service for the Mentally Ill*[1]

For months and years during his late twenties, Jay wandered. Various menial jobs led nowhere. Peer group friends disappeared. Eventually left on his own, our son rambled about in his home suburban community. Waitresses in local restaurants expressed concern for the solitary guest seated, smoking, at all hours of the day beside the coffee mug they kept replenishing. Sometimes he visited the local public library and heard tapes. Alcohol imbibed during tavern visits—given his medication regimen—was threatening his stability, but at least he managed to stay out of trouble.

This lifestyle put those of us at home on edge, but it remained, at least on a day-to-day basis, a tolerable association. Jay seemed to understand that if he continued to sustain himself like this he could still count on family for indefinite support as well as for rescue at hospital relapse times. As I have already suggested, we had welcomed this standoff as a "balm in Gilead" and as a basis for hope in "crossing the Jordan" to possess the land of renewal and hope.

Looking back, however, it was a period embracing our unspoken denial of desperate realities. In this chapter I will explain why, by sketching two additional anecdotes that underscore our actual vulnerability and need for outside intervention. We could fool ourselves no longer about managing our fragile adult child while at the same time sustaining ordinary living demands and job routines. When we needed it most—like ancient Israel in its desert journey—we were granted the gift of a promised land. God employed a therapist and respite caregivers to redeem and save.

Therapist

Looking good had long since escaped Jay's attention. Little by little, we adjusted to his disheveled appearance quite beyond collegiate standards for "casual." Not much surprised me. Yet one afternoon I was taken aback when we happened to meet on the street near his tiny apartment. He wore what looked like a splint on the outside lower leg of the baggy bib overalls.

"Jay, what is that?" I asked as he drew nearer.

"I need it for protection, Dad," he replied, and produced a razor-sharp, two-edged military survival knife. (Lunacy at large, I sighed to myself.)

The splint was its sheath, attached by large rubber bands. He must have been scraping up funds for the lethal-looking object for some time.

"But Jay," I warned, "carrying a knife like that must be illegal."

"Oh, no, it isn't," he said, and silently I searched for ideas of how I could separate the weapon from its paranoid owner. Little wonder the Asian refugees sharing his apartment building—as I would learn later—were afraid of their neighbor, who was usually alone and walking the streets late at night.

Even so, Ann and I, together with counselors at our community mental health center, still hoped that "independence" for Jay at this stage was a necessary step toward recovery and healing.

One night an event in the tumult of these months showed how things had finally gotten out of hand. It happened on Sunday, and I had taught an adult church school class in a congregation an hour's drive away. As he had done a few times before, Jay rode along (staying in the car during church), and we stopped for lunch afterward. At the economy cafeteria in the city center I called him—quite mildly, I thought—on rude behavior in the line. He had no answer. We said little on the rest of the way home, and early in the afternoon I dropped him off at his two-room apartment.

At home once more, I reported an uneventful trip to Ann and Erin, puttered around the yard, and at dusk settled down for some television football. Tired after a long day, I decided to retire a bit early. The still-on bedroom television, mixed with conversation from the kitchen, only increased my drowsiness.

The doorbell jarred my ears, and I heard more conversation. The front door opened, and the next moment Jay burst into the bedroom. The ludicrous Stetson hat pulled low on his forehead capped an accusing finger: "You talk to me through my head," he snarled. Then, before I could reply, he grabbed my chest with both hands and bounced me up and down, and I felt a fist hit my face.

Erin reached the bedroom first to grab him from behind: "Jay, Jay!" The dark figure pulled back.

"You've hurt Dad!" she cried.

"Oh, I *have not*." He sounded matter-of-fact.

Somehow his sister and mother moved the intruder out the front door and quickly turned the dead bolt behind him.

Blood warmed my face, and I could see it spattering the sheets. The fractured nose offered no pain at the time, but in minutes we were on our way to the nearest hospital emergency room.

His rage, I thought, must have resulted from my trivial rebuff at the cafeteria. Then it hit me. "The survival knife," I said to myself, "he hadn't worn it to church today." I knew I was lucky. In just minutes a turning point had been reached. The involuntary hospital commitment criterion, "a danger to oneself or others," took life. I finally admitted to myself that our family, Jay's primary caregivers at that time, needed help.

Pacific Community Mental Health Center (PCMHC) staff and Dr. H., Jay's psychiatrist, took over. "You're looking at a long-term commitment, Jay," declared the doctor, "for we're not going to put up with violence." Evidently Jay had now passed the commitment criterion test. The specter of a locked-up situation at Fir Lane State Hospital was apparently enough to give pause, and Dr. H's patient took up residence at a congregate care facility (CCF) arranged for through the PCMHC. We were at the end of our rope, and the mental health system defined just the support we needed. We had been lucky, I suppose, for from that time he seemed to get more focused attention. But it can work out differently in other families.

My research shows that if a son or daughter becomes ill as a teenager and is covered by a parent's insurance, in the initial phase he or she will in all probability be treated. As the illness recurs, however, families feel the impact of the "least restrictive setting" barrier established by the mental health bar. They discover that an individual who is not "dangerous" cannot be treated against her or his will. And how is "dangerous" defined? Must the prospective client either attempt suicide or threaten the interviewer to qualify? Moreover, if the individual *is* judged to be dangerous, and is treated, he or she will in all probability be released from the hospital in a matter of days.[2] The catch-22 problem accelerates when, with a diseased brain, many will not wish to have anything to do with hospitals because they do not consider themselves "psycho ward" candidates in the slightest. The "revolving door" carousel (treatment, premature release, acute stage, and treatment again) spins ever faster.

Jay's congregate care facility was a modest house on the edge of the city's industrial zone, and eight other men and women resided there at the time. Discipline, rules, and regulations were absolute, yet every resident was legally free to walk away at any time and try once more on his or her own. For most, however, this would mean housing on the streets. The care also included attention to medical needs. Because a common side effect of one of his medications was dry mouth, resulting in a lack of saliva and devastating tooth decay, Ann and I had given up on scheduling and paying for dental attention long ago. Therapy allies decided to supervise the removal of Jay's teeth and the obtaining of dentures.[3]

Jay decided to make the CCF Start Over House his home. Its rules about mealtime attendance and evening curfews were his. Later on, I touched base over the telephone and supplied an occasional carton of cigarettes. Regulated medication, a proper diet, and psychotherapy including group counseling would work small wonders. For example, when I overhear parents take just pride in the graduations, promotions, and other accomplishments of their offspring, I have become able to say to myself, "Well, recently my thirty-four-year-old son, all by himself, took the city bus to pay us a visit. Good for him!" Is this a joke? Not at all if he happens to have been diagnosed with a chronic mental disorder. (Yet how can it be, I ask myself, that in recent years I have moved from feelings of anger, fear, and frustration to sentiments of empathy and compassion?) He has now lived away from home for more than ten years. Family-sponsored outings—usually a car ride, home visit (never overnight), or shopping tour—complement a circle of care.

"Home is the place where, when you have to go there," writes the poet, "they have to take you in." Sorry, Mr. Frost, not this time.[4]

Advocate

One time I invited him along to a local mall. When he slipped into the car, I noticed he had not shaved. Strands of unwashed hair filtered through along the brim of the ever-present Greek fisherman's cap perched on his brow. It looked (and smelled) as if he had slept in his clothes the past few days as well.

No one seemed to notice us in the crowds until we entered a record shop. The classical tape section I sought was at the back of the room and, with Jay hovering at my side, I began to search for Christmas carol music. Meanwhile my partner began to pace a bit. I watched from the corner of my eye and decided he would be needing another cigarette before long.

Just then a man asked if he could help. I gladly accepted and told him what I was looking for. Instead of leading the way for his customer, however, he abruptly disappeared. Puzzled, I waited but then decided it was time to head for the parking lot anyway.

We sauntered along the store fronts until my son bolted ahead, as he often did, seeking (I surmise) the cozy security of the car once more. He walked with his customary quick, mechanical step that is probably a medication side effect. The crowds, I guessed, had been too much to bear. By now the mall exit door was in view, and I paused to put on my hat and coat against the rainy night outside. Jay turned and waited for me at the door.

Next, to my surprise, he offered one of the two or three sentences of conversation up to that time. "Dad," he called in a loud voice, "it looks like we've got trouble here." I turned to see two armed security men approach.

"Would you show your IDs?"

Jay pulled out his wallet to display his prized city bus pass, and I, without thinking, offered my driver's license and university faculty card.

"We want to ask you some questions." People paused in the fast food eating areas, and several stared from the theater entrance nearby.

The music store clerk—evidently the manager—appeared next. One of the officers moved, menacingly, behind us. Our accuser, pointing in Jay's direction, then announced his opinion that "he" (not my companion, friend, or partner) had been in his office back at the store. Jay shook his head.

By this time, livid with anger, I picked up my son's use of the term "trouble" moments before. Moving up to the officer who had asked for our identifications, I blurted, "I recently returned from a semester's teaching and travel in the People's Republic of China. Not once did any police officer, soldier, or official over there ask for my ID like this. We are in the United States of America. Do you want trouble?"

I turned to the manager, "Search us!" Looking him in the eye, I continued, "Do you want me to call my attorney? Do *you* want trouble?" Silence.

Moments later we continued our trek to the parking lots. Sober-faced as usual, Jay muttered an ironic, "That was funny, Dad." I could not agree. Inwardly I excused what I took to be inexperienced and poorly trained security guards. In contrast, the manager had punctured the facade of my personal accommodation to our son's illness and released the winds of resentment at Jay's outsiderhood. Feelings of frustration surfaced in public. Then I recognized something else: I had become an advocate. By speaking out, I had allied myself with mental health system professionals in confronting public stigma surrounding mental illness.

On the way back to Start Over House, I silently numbered us among all those nameless folks who must endure far greater slights for having deviated from expected appearance, dress, and behavior standards. Jay, I suppose, had fit neatly into the accuser's "thief" and "threat" profile. Had the complainer only understood that in his moment of frightened pacing back at the shop, my companion would not even have had the courage to *open* the office door, much less to pilfer the room's contents.

Jay at least was in good company, I thought to myself when recalling another Outsider. "Foxes have holes, and birds of the air have nests," said Jesus, "but the Son of Man has nowhere to lay his head" (Luke 9:58).

Respite

The question of housing persists as one of our nation's greatest unmet social service needs. From many groups—legislators, families, minorities, and clinicians—comes the plea for *adequate housing*. In addition, the media routinely lament the scandalous and humiliating situations put up with by homeless citizens who sleep in parks, shelters, doorways, and cars. Many of them appear to me to be wilderness refugees.

One person, open Bible in hand, paces alongside the busy avenue as he preaches to scurrying autos. Another—scowling and bareheaded in the rain—shuffles on a path to nowhere. Without fail she will curse you for making eye contact, even from your car. In prior times perhaps both might have found refuge in asylums. I have noticed them repeatedly during recent months in our neighborhood.

Up to now we had not set the agenda. Rather, for the most part, we had simply reacted to Jay's problems and looked hopefully toward what would prove to be one piecemeal housing arrangement after another: the state hospital, psych wards at public hospitals, a private psychiatric hospital, and (through PCMHC) partially supervised living quarters. Various roommates and single-occupancy situations rounded out our continued experiments with "adequate housing" (see figure 3).

In terms of treatment and rehabilitation, however, our love or bonding with Jay left our family with a threat of full reengagement by default. Lack of information sharing by the hospital and of followups by either hospital or community mental health personnel could speed the drift toward victimizing the family. We still lack the capacity to function as a kind of outside-the-hospital ward attendant. Our concern is not unusual by comparison to other families in a similar situation.[5]

Alliances, newly discovered, brought confidence. Together with therapists and respite caregivers, we could face the indefinite "sustaining" issues: (1) Jay's carelessness in following medication directions, (2) fragmented therapeutic support lacking any clear and long-term treatment plan, and (3) our family's ignorance of serious mental illness in general, its causes, symptoms, and prognosis.[6]

Start Over House had offered stabilization and respite, the first hint

Living Arrangements	Effect on Child	Effect on Parent	Result
Jail Streets	Destruction	Despair	Parent/ child Victims
Hospital Private Public	Short-term stabilization	Respite Hope in medicine	Short- term intervention
Home	Respite	Burden Disruption Tension	Mixed success and failure
Congregate care facility	Long-term stabilization	Support Respite Teamwork/ health professionals	Long- term intervention

FIG. 3. MENTAL ILLNESS HOUSING

of teamwork potential with health professionals and our family, plus a successful long-term intervention. But what next? Dare we contemplate an end to the heartache? Was this the last resort? Could Jay ever make it on his own? How about rehabilitation? Was recovery an impossible dream on the part of his caregivers? We would revel in the respite but entertain hope for solutions.

PART THREE
Letting Go

8
Giving Sorrow
Words

Give sorrow words: the grief that does not speak, whispers to the
over-burdened heart and bids it break.

—Shakespeare, *Macbeth,* IV, 3

Our thirty-four-year-old son has come home for a visit. There he sits,
cross-legged on the grass, in the middle of the backyard. At night a
cigarette glow betrays the silent vigil in the very same spot. Sometimes he mutters and shouts under his breath but certainly means no
harm.

It is a rather new thing, this ritual. Like the now familiar Greek
fisherman's cap he began wearing two years ago, it adds to the private
list of eccentric habits I have witnessed in recent years. What next? I
ask myself. Why so exactly in the middle of the yard? Should I laugh
or cry? What about the utter absurdity of it all? On a deeper level, is
our visitor, this somber guru, actually our Jay? Isn't insanity reserved
for folks we would rather not think about, hidden from sight in state
hospitals?

Once more the urge to deny everything presses in on me. As if
engaged by a switch I can never seem to locate, grief has tagged along
with the guest.

"To have a chronically ill loved one is indescribably painful," la-
ments another parent, for "the anguish may subside at times but it
never really goes away." When periods of stability and improvement
occur, a relapse lurks behind; hence, "to have hope revived, then

dashed, is the cruelest kind of grief."[1] Most of us associate the emotion with mourning at the death of a loved one. In *Good Grief,* Granger Westberg calls attention to loss at the center of things: Grief is what happens to us when we lose connections with persons or matters that are vitally important in our lives.[2]

Possibly only those directly involved can embrace the particularities of suffering various burdens of affliction. A New Testament Greek word, *lypē,* may read as "grief" or "pain" in English; Peter, for example, "felt hurt" when Jesus challenged his loyalty a third time (John 21:17).[3] Paul intensifies the interpretation by separating a "godly" grief that leads to repentance from a "worldly" grief that "produces death" (2 Cor. 7:10). I attach the whole concept of human suffering to my translation; pain can assault both mind and body. Grief emotions may even seem to threaten the very core of one's being. They can produce utterances like "I'm going to pieces" or "He's falling apart." Mental illness symptoms in a young adult can bring family members close to such feelings. I shake my head in sympathy with another father confronted by an untimely death in the family.

At the death of his son Eric, a twenty-five-year-old killed in an Austrian mountain-climbing accident, Nicholas Wolterstorff shares the inner pain of grief and loss. Despite consolers who remind him of the hope of resurrection, he cries out,

> Yet Eric is gone, *here* and *now* he is gone; *now* I cannot talk with him, *now* I cannot see him, *now* I cannot hug him, *now* I cannot hear of his plans for the future. That is my sorrow.

Loss, separation, and grief—how many parents have tasted similar pain. Hence the author has bared his soul "in the hope that it will be of help to some of those who find themselves with us in the company of mourners."[4]

I find myself in their number, too, but having a different burden:

> I can *talk with Jay,* but only in simple sentences, and after having initiated any exchange. Small talk is unwelcome. (Anyone for apathy?) I can *see him,* all right, in his thrift store clothing outfit, and behind the scruffy beard notice he has neglected once more to put in his false teeth. I also notice he needs a shower. And there's the visored black cap, as always, carefully in place—indoors, outdoors, rain or shine. (Dr. H. allows that he is hiding behind beard and cap.)

There are also limits:

I *cannot hug my son* because the medications—or whatever else the cause—make body boundaries indefinite, and he'd rather not touch. I *cannot help but wince* when I hear the hacking cough as I hand over another "treat," a death-dealing carton of cigarettes; and I *cannot testify* to others of his plans for the future because he doesn't make any.

My sorrow is a bit different, then, because the Jay seated before me will never erase a previous picture of the quite "verbal" (a term from various counseling sessions) teenager who a few years back so easily met the public in his part-time restaurant job and who posed proudly on a newly purchased motorcycle. Plans for the future abounded. That Jay is gone. My bitterness wants to reverse the "born anew" experience (John 3:3, RSV). Mine is not "from above," but from below; not for the better, but for the worse.

Now, quiet and unobtrusive, he does not bother anyone—another dividend, I suppose, of the deinstitutionalization movement. Still, I must admit to feeling a kinship with the mother who writes about her twenty-eight-year-old son with mental illness.

So unless he commits an outwardly violent act, my son gets listed as a "success." . . . That is not how he looks to me. I think he looks like a giant, broken plastic, throwaway toy. And he breaks my heart.[5]

Our tribe of parents has *loss* in common, but the pain comes in different packages. Think of the parents of suicides, I remind myself, and of murdered or missing children. Why should I or anyone else be immune from joining their fellowship? The answer is negative, of course, but with an important postscript: Although my grief is alive and resists the psychological working-through task, I do not have to become a victim of it.

Endurance: Three Bible Scenarios

King David, epic Bible hero, nearly became a casualty of grief. Late in his career domestic troubles began to mount and his son Absalom seized power. As civil war erupted, the king was forced to flee his own country (2 Samuel 15–19). Yet, gathering enough loyal troops together, the monarch achieved a reversal of fortunes and victory over the rebels.

Despite the family betrayal, Joab, commander of the king's forces, had been cautioned to protect the defiant Absalom (18:12). Instead, the general murdered the prince as he dangled from a tree with his head caught in its limbs (18:14–15). Afterward, the court historian reveals the poignant, human side of this legendary parent as he describes the ruler's lament upon the news of Absalom's death:

> The King was deeply moved, and went up to the chamber over the gate, and wept; and as he went, he said, "O my son Absalom, my son, my son Absalom! Would I had died instead of you, O Absalom, my son, my son!" (2 Sam. 18:33)

So profound was the agony of the king's ordeal that even military victory celebrations were now forgotten; he had lost touch with public duty. In a bizarre twist, a hard-earned festivity was about to become a day of mourning for the enemy. Joab senses the crisis at hand. Approaching the stricken monarch, he both scolds him and offers practical advice:

> Today you have covered with shame the faces of all your officers, who have saved your life today . . . for love of those who hate you and for hatred of those who love you. . . . I perceive that if Absalom were alive and all of us were dead today, then you would be pleased. So go out at once and speak kindly to your servants . . . if you do not go, not a man will stay with you this night; and this will be worse for you than any disaster that has come upon you. (2 Sam. 19:5–7)

Just as on a previous turning point involving adultery and murder (1 Samuel 11–12), David accepted both the intervention and the counsel. He decided to act—refusing to let grief isolate him any longer—and went out to meet his subjects. The king would still serve the covenant-making God despite his own failures in maintaining its bond. Eventually it all came down to the soul-searching prayer, "a broken and contrite heart, O God, you will not despise" (Ps. 51:17). David had survived his troubles; grief had had its day. At the very end, therefore, the battle-weary warrior could exult, "By my God I can leap over a wall" (2 Sam. 22:30).

A prophet of Israel provides a second biblical insight for connecting grief and endurance. Things were going well for God's people Israel in the eighth century before Christ. Affluence and military security were apparent benefits of public policy and worship at official shrines.

An uncouth shepherd from Tekoa, who likely had come north to Jerusalem to sell animals at the Bethel shrine, voiced a different view. Compelled by a call from the Lord (Amos 3:3–8), Amos denounced the sanctuary piety there as vain; true faithfulness to God's covenant, he cried, meant that no one should be rich at the expense of the poor and marginalized (2:6–8; 5:21–24). Without repentance, judgment would come in the form of an Assyrian army attack (2:13–16). Meanwhile, his listeners traveled the same old path: party time and empty ritual (4:1–5). Persistent although rejected, the prophet grieved. He had seen the big picture; in truth, disaster had befallen those from whom so much more might be expected: "Alas for those who lie upon beds of ivory . . . who sing idle songs to the sound of the harp . . . who drink wine from bowls . . . but are not grieved over the ruin of Joseph!" (Amos 6:4–6).

Yet the ultimate vision of the prophet is not defeat and doom; judgment was not to be an end in itself. God would provide life and renewal for a "remnant" of those who in repenting would seek righteousness and justice: "I will restore the fortunes of my people Israel" (9:14). Centuries later another angry prophet would grieve for those who could not look beyond the immediate. He nevertheless went on to "do good" and heal in an act of pure mercy and compassion (Mark 3:4–5). Can God's ultimate grace—as difficult to believe in as it sometimes appears—also belong in the big picture for those of us struggling with the grief of mental illness?

The third context I use to examine the content of endurance takes note of a bit of advice from a letter Paul wrote to one of his first congregations. Faith in God, he declares, means that believers should not grieve "as others do who have no hope" (1 Thess. 4:13). Surely there must have been situations in which grief was experienced. Yet the apostle's counsel concerns grieving with a "plus." We must always cultivate hope.

"Neither in presumption nor in despair lies the power to renew our life," writes a leading Protestant theologian, "but only in the hope that is enduring and sure."[6] So what can hope for such quality of life imply in our peculiar circumstances? Will it be denial or wishful thinking all over again, merely on a more respectable religious level? Because chronic mental illness abides in our families, do we never really relate to each other like neighbors in normal broods? Are we only *hoping* to live? My answer is no. Christian hope can make us ready to bear the cross of even these realities. Our God can make all things new (2 Cor. 5:17) and create from nothing once more. "Hope . . . pronounces the poor blessed, receives the weary and heavy laden, the humbled and the wronged . . . it goes on its way through the midst of happiness and pain."[7]

As hope explores a pilgrimage road, so also will blessing. A divine vision of long ago declares blessed (happy, fortunate) those who persevere until the "end of days" (Dan. 12:12–13). To be blessed provides a means to share God's ageless purposes of grace. Hear the psalmist's call to hang on: suddenly the author, while bemoaning his trouble (Ps. 77:1–9), finds a new resource of blessing. He recalls the Lord's deeds in history, the exodus, and all its subsequent miracles (vv. 11–20). For him the holy God of such great wonders could become more than a match for his sorrow. Grief was transformed (v. 10).

If up to now I have depicted rather grand but vague generalities— wonder of the holiness of God, the big picture, and hope—it is because benefits within various activities of ordinary life are at the same time inspired from them. One writer observes, "God works slowly, and he often accomplishes his purposes in life's little events. . . . Our faithfulness cannot always be realized through programs of epic proportions. We are called to be obedient where we are located, with the resources available to us, and in the light of our present understanding of God's will."[8] Let the struggle of our family with the chronic illness of one of its members serve to illustrate a few specifics of this claim.

Small Wonders

Our guest out on the lawn has finished lunch with us and is about to leave for "home," the inner city house he shares with two other men, fellow clients of the local mental health center social club. It represents an experimental new living arrangement with more independence. The housemates also are under supervised medication procedures. Jay's polite thank you joins with our promise to keep in touch. Transformed, the posturing out on the lawn becomes a moment of healing.

Among our other encounters of the previous eighteen years are many we never would have chosen, but in God's power we have been strengthened "to endure everything with patience while joyfully giving thanks" (Col. 1:11). Let me apply these elements of strength from reflections about our family's firsthand knowledge.

Endurance

Studies show that people who are psychiatrically disabled rarely accept community-based treatment programs after hospital stays. In one study, two thirds of the patients referred to an outpatient setting failed to appear for help. Moreover, even with some self-selection of settings, dropout rates in certain areas exceeded fifty percent during the first nine months.[9] At our house we have held our breath for more than five years as Jay has not only accepted community-based treatment but also advanced to more personal independence within it. Still, on any given day—as so frequently happened before—he may simply walk away from it all.

This means endurance *for him* as well: faithfulness in taking those pills on a daily basis and maintaining harmony with his housemates, the latter a formidable challenge for lots of "normal" folks. Above all else it means he must avoid alcohol. He never mentions private battles with these affairs, yet if he should go "off" again we would be among the first to learn about any setback.

Patience

We are thankful for the big-picture capabilities of mental health professionals who have played the role of Joab for us. That they also assisted Jay to secure a city bus pass—and encouraged him to muster the courage to use it—was a marvel. When later he notified us he had lost the pass, we let it remain *his* problem, although intervention on our part might have been easier than the suspense of waiting (it took weeks) to arrange for a duplicate. Keeping psychiatric and blood-level test appointments are more serious matters, but seldom do we intervene to assure connections. Jay "owns" the problem.

My problem is understanding him better and seeing him for what he is today. Could it be true that in these years so full of crises, fears, hospitals, seedy apartments, and frustrations God has been at hand after all? Yes, I answer. God is the one who has pushed me, prodded me, and opened my eyes. I have been stretched to the limit, yet also comforted. Through those years I have come to know Jay and a few of his associates like Tony as candidates one day to illustrate the Lord's prediction about the age to come: "But many who are first will be last, and the last will be first" (Mark 10:31) and surely numbered among "the least" in the King's family (Matt. 25:31–46). In these least understood, tolerated, and served fellow citizens, a strange but more meaningful vision of the cross borne by their brother Jesus has come to light.

Joy

For Paul joy is a product of being with Christ in his cause (see Philippians). While I celebrate this grand vision, I also relish the cheer surrounding little events.

Have you ever seen someone, minus false teeth, have a go at a hot piece of pizza? We sat by a modest mall fast-food counter (Jay's preference) and chuckled together at his eating effort. It was his thirty-fourth birthday party, and our laughter made me realize how much better things had become. His party was a simple affair, but he was pleased. Consider a thirty-something young man, an "anti-yuppie" with no car, no job or certificate or degree, and no permanent place to call his own. Did any of the great ones—the Buddha, Jesus, Francis of Assisi, Gandhi—I ask myself, travel with much more? Jay *appreciates* a good meal and a clean shirt. Does he actually belong in the company of the poor who in Christ's eyes someday will hear *good news* (Luke 4:18)?

There is also hope in joy. A research professor of psychiatry, Leona Bachrach, has worked through patients' writings that deal with their self-understanding. She discovered much emphasis on the idea that where there is no hope there can be no improvement. One patient found joy in music, but then came the voices:

> During orchestra practice one day the voices were badgering me with endless taunts and criticisms, further rattling me by singing the music a half a bar ahead of where we were playing. I couldn't concentrate on playing my cello. The orchestra played on, while I struggled to reestablish my place in the music. It was too much. Uncontrollable tears welled up in my eyes and spilled over. The

more I tried to stop my crying and pay attention to the music, the faster the tears streamed down my cheeks.[10]

Increasingly, family support groups in partnership with competent and caring professionals are rolling back such craziness. Furthermore, some of us who grieve in our unique way can find solace in the promise, "Blessed are those who mourn, for they will be comforted" (Matt. 5:4). Until then, the pain continues and sometimes hurts so much we can also find our burdens lightened by doing something about it.

9

Reframing

But Joseph said to [his brothers], "Do not be afraid! Am I in the place of God? Even though you intended to do harm to me, God intended it for good . . . as he is doing today. So have no fear."

—Genesis 50:19–21

Is the glass containing water there on the table half-empty or half-full? You have a choice in framing your reply; if "half-full," you connect with potential and optimism. Bouts with schizophrenia put me in a half-empty frame of mind, I admit, but a half-full attitude will undergird the rest of what I have to say about surviving serious mental illness in the family.

Did you ever notice how Jesus reframes ordinary perceptions? "Blessed are the meek, for they will inherit the earth" (Matt. 5:5). To me it still looks as though the rich, the celebrities, and the powerful have an edge. And we are to rejoice when, as disciples, we are *reviled* and *persecuted* (Matt. 5:11)? To "reframe" means to "change the conceptual and/or emotional setting or viewpoint in relation to which a situation is experienced and to place it in another frame which fits the 'facts' of the same concrete situation equally well or even better, and thereby changes its entire meaning."[1]

Take a radical example. Caught up in the Holocaust, Viktor Frankl suffered the loss of family, civil rights, profession, and—given a branded number on his skin—even his name. At last, in the prison showers, he was told to shave his body; reduced to a vulnerable, naked self, he took hold of one last possession the persecutors could not reach: his attitude toward these events. He chose to reframe death camp horror into a will to survive. After the war he shared the story in *Man's Search for Meaning*. "Not only creativeness and enjoyment are meaningful," he insists, for "if there is a meaning in life at all, then there must be meaning in suffering. . . . Without suffering and death human life cannot be complete."[2]

Learning to Pray

What a way to spend an afternoon. Jay had called, wanting to go out for coffee. "He sounded really good," I announced to Ann, and left on the twenty-minute drive across town to join him.

The skies were clear and the temperature balmy when Jay appeared at the car door with a pleasant hello. Gently I suggested he would not need the winter cap and down-filled vest he wore over his sweatshirt. But no, so I let it go as "his problem." The drive was pleasant enough—no talk, just radio rock music—and before long we slid into a cafeteria smoking-section booth. As usual, only necessary words were exchanged, but I had long since accepted the benefit of our mutual presence in the humble enjoyment of food and drink.

Then it began: deep, muttering drags on the cigarette, rubbing the wristwatch face, rocking, and feet-shuffling.

"Are you okay?" No answer—by now my companion was entirely occupied with listening to Someone Else.

"Let's get going, Jay."

"No. I'm okay. I'll go outside and smoke."

Alone and relieved to notice that not many people seemed to be around, I lingered over dessert and coffee. Outside again, I spotted him thirty yards distant. People about to enter their cars paused by the open doors and gaped. Several youths loitering near the cafe door fell silent.

Red-faced, with contorted countenance and a white knuckled fist at his side (the other hand maintained the burning tobacco), Jay was yelping passionately to the Other(s), sort of under his breath, oblivious to everything else. "Encore time," I decided during my approach. "Time for another 'subvocal' happening." This senseless self-absorption moved on a plane of torment completely hidden from his caregiver father and the parking lot spectators. After an interlude of stomping around (with me in tow) we paraded—no wonder people stared—to our car and, in sweaty, silent despair, made it back to the house without even testing the boundary of "no smoking in the car."

Should I have tried to explain the bizarre behavior—beginning with deinstitutionalization perhaps—to our fellow citizens on the parking lot? What a chance to apply the "educate the public" cliché! Not really; I had no stomach for it, only a sickening dismay, surprisingly alive after so many years. The unpredictable outburst left me disgusted and angry. All the care, treatment, and love of parents, siblings, relatives and friends, health professionals, clerics, counselors, social workers, educators, and other advocates had come down to this: an awesome adult rage or tantrum. However, after thinking it over, I decided I should no more fault him for having a brain abnormality than I should fault a diabetic for a diseased pancreas. Perhaps a format of meaning for this suffering can still appear, I found myself thinking.

The ancient Greek word *mainomai* (source of the English "maniac") means to "rage" or "be furious."[3] I had seen it before. It was getting easier for me to understand Matthew's depiction of the Canaanite woman. She pleaded to the visitor in her country named Jesus, "Have mercy on me, Lord, Son of David; my daughter is tormented by a demon" (Matt. 15:22). Familiar utterances from the Psalms also struck home:

> How long, O Lord? Will you forget me forever?
> How long will you hide your face from me?
> How long must I bear pain in my soul,
> and have sorrow in my heart all day long? . . .
>
> (Ps. 13:1–2)

I had long been aware that familiar lines from the Psalter define both poetry and faith ("The Lord is my shepherd"). But now I recognized the *prayers,* pleas from real people who also groaned in spirit:

> Out of the depths I cry to you, O Lord,
> Lord, hear my voice!
> Let your ears be attentive
> to the voice of my supplications!
>
> (Ps. 130:1–2)

Luke's portrait of Jesus as a person of prayer also merged with the fatigue I began to notice after incidents like this one. He prayed, for instance, all night long at a time of crisis; only then did he choose the Twelve (6:12–16). So I too could certainly pray for guidance. Jesus would also withdraw from the crowds for private prayer (5:16; 9:18, 28) and anticipated guidance as a result. I decided it would be good to reframe so much of my dependence on research and counseling toward a more disciplined regimen of prayer. Furthermore, I remembered an intercessory prayer on behalf of Simon (Luke 22:32). It reminded me of my growing awareness of how in church one rarely hears prayer on behalf of those suffering from mental illness and their families. If there are other particulars in congregational "prayer requests," why are there not also mentions of those grappling with such problems? Justified or not, affected families would rather sometimes avoid attention because of the shame represented by presumed emotional failures in their midst. It takes courage to step out from the margins of guilt and shame. Possibly the old-fashioned term "repentance" applies even better than reframing. Let the contours of a classic biblical story point a way to the spiritual strength I was seeking.

A Case Story: Job

His world had come apart. Bereaved, impoverished, and with his health imperiled, Job nevertheless endured. Many readers salute this model of patience whose piety persists without loss of faith (1:1–2:13; 42:7–17; James 5:11). Yet in the poetic section—the main part of the book—the pathetic figure atop the ash heap is *anything but* patient. In the crucible of suffering he curses the day of his birth and hurls protests against God who had taken away the purpose of life. The furious Job is defiant and unwilling to relinquish his claim that God, not he, is responsible for his plight. God is to blame, and Job demands a hearing.[4]

Three visitors to the scene of suffering were unable to console the sufferer with faith notions based on conventional wisdom. First comes the notion that suffering is God's own gracious course of education (chaps. 4, 5, and 8), which had produced Job's inappropriate posture of rebellion against God's leading (chap. 15). Then, the patriarch is accused of pride before the Almighty, having evidently even rejected prayer and worship as avenues for peace with God (chaps. 22, 25, and 33). Amid a series of overlapping arguments, a common uniting factor seems to be the "doctrinal theology" perspective. (Can rigorous theological pursuit result in distancing *experience* from a passion for answers?)

Chapter 28 poses a critical question: "Where, then, does wisdom come from?" (vv. 12, 20). One interpreter suggests two directions for an answer. The first looks back to previous chapters where truth resides in the natural order of things. Observing the dependability of God's created order reinforces our overall experience of a constant, regular, and reliable world (see Gen. 1:1–2:4a and 8:20–22).

> As long as the earth endures,
> seedtime and harvest, cold and heat,
> summer and winter, day and night,
> shall not cease.

> (Gen. 8:22)

The second direction points forward to chaps. 29–31. Here Job's militant posture asserts that answers to unjust suffering will not be forced after all; God *withholds* more than he discloses. The scope of inquiry broadens to the question asking if any meaningful human contact with God is even possible, given the unjustly suffering creature. Job wonders how anyone can deal with a Creator who deliberately withholds crucial knowledge in such a fashion.[5]

The bible of the American Psychiatric Association, *Diagnostic and Statistical Manual of Mental Disorders, Third Edition Revised* (*DSM-IIIR*) puts my questions about God, mental illness, and religious faith into a secular format. This text avoids labeling persons like Jay as "insane" or "crazy." A *mental disorder* has taken hold. The authors conceive this as

> a clinically significant behavioral or psychological syndrome or pattern that occurs in a person and that is associated with present distress (a painful symptom) or disability (impairment in one or more important areas of functioning) or with a significantly increased risk of suffering death, pain, disability, or an important loss of freedom. . . . Whatever its original cause, it must currently be considered a manifestation of a behavioral, psychological, or biological dysfunction in the person.[6]

Nineteen major classifications of disorder are listed, including (1) those first evident in infancy, childhood, or adolescence; (2) organic mental disorders (including the Alzheimer type); (3) schizophrenia;

(4) psychoactive substance abuse disorders; and (5) anxiety disorders. Scores of subclassifications are identified. Still, none of these classifications addresses the bottom line of suffering—both for the one in whom the disorder appears and among those who love him or her—belonging to the quest for "religious reality."

How can a loving, all-powerful God tolerate all this? Does the *deity* inflict suffering? In the Old Testament, God (Yahweh) has entered into a relationship of patronage with Israel (Ex. 3:6–10; 24:11); it is counted among God's possessions. God saves and blesses the people. Any break in the relationship of trust, any turning away of Yahweh from the people, is equivalent in meaning to decline and suffering. From a distance and by looking back through the means of historical interpretation, readers can sort out the times of suffering endured by individuals and nations. Still, other voices, like Job's, read between the lines and show how in the *present*—as in the case of my acute distress out in the parking lot—the rim of suffering seems only to expand.[7] Job never denies God's reality but he *fears God's arbitrariness.* Are the ways of God either fair or consistent? Can they really make sense to us? As far as the sufferings arising from mental disorders are concerned, I am tempted to say no.

One reason is the unique sense of meaninglessness ("craziness") in various episodes shared with my son. Another is the severity of the disabling condition itself, one that seems to strike at the core of Jay's very being and transform him into another person, a young adult with such a profound, joyless apathy (medication side effects?). To me, mental illness carries an ultimate: it hints at the yawning, formless void present at the beginning before God's wind swept over and brought light to original disorder (Gen. 1:1–3). If other parents and "consumers" in the mental health system avoided protests similar to Job's, we could suffer even more, namely, spiritual loss and defeat. Where there is lament, there is at least life. Similar to the story of Israel, our partnership with a covenant-making God, although veiled, creates a constant summons to hope between the polarities of sorrow and praise. We learn to reframe the anger.

Christ Disabled

Bible study can both sharpen the pain and frame the heartache. After Jesus healed Peter's mother-in-law (Matt. 8:14–16), the evangelist comments, "This was to fulfill what had been spoken through the prophet Isaiah, 'He took our infirmities and bore our diseases'" (Matt. 8:17).

What can Matthew mean? He has quoted a passage from Isaiah's Suffering Servant imagery (52:13–53:12). Yet here, and according to other New Testament witnesses, stands the very One chosen by God—the disabled Christ?—who has taken our infirmities (handi-capping conditions) and shouldered our diseases (schizophrenia). The book of Hebrews reminds believers of a Jesus who "in every respect has been tested" as the rest of us are, yet is without sin (4:15). Our fellow sufferer also humbled and "emptied himself" (Phil. 2:6–11). Who among us, I ask, can experience more testing and humiliation than persons like Jay who must contest with those tormenting voices of auditory hallucinations? The disabled Christ, I answer, who stands side by side with them.

Such a claim reverberates in the words of an early twentieth-century theologian at the close of *The Quest of the Historical Jesus:*

> He comes to us as One unknown, without a name, as of old, by the lakeside, He came to those men who knew Him not. He speaks to us the same word: "Follow thou me!" and sets us to the tasks which He has to fulfill for our time. He commands. And to those who obey Him, whether they be wise or simple, He will reveal Himself in the toils, the conflicts, the sufferings which they shall pass through in His fellowship, and as an ineffable mystery, they shall learn in their own experience Who He is.[8]

As Schweitzer notes, those who learn to have fellowship with the mysterious leader will experience "toils, conflicts, and sufferings," not the comfort-enhancing prizes wrapped up in recognition and achievement.

Besides reframing my normative emphasis on the risen Christ and Lord, life within limits has become a vital reality and slowed down my pursuit of religious and psychological crutches. Anger recedes and the strangest reframing of all has taken place: rebirth within the boundaries of God's salvation.[9] Lament has given voice to suffering and becomes the means to approach the One who can take it away. It spurs a movement toward God.[10]

Several years ago Ann and I prepared to board a train at the Frank-furt station in Germany. Over the crowd I heard someone singing the hymn "Amazing Grace." "Another panhandler," I guessed. But a short time later another refrain caught my ear:

> Let the whole creation cry,
> "Glory to the Lord on high!"
> Heaven and earth, awake and sing,
> "Praise him, our almighty King!"
> Praise him, angel hosts above,
> Ever bright and fair in love;
> Sun and moon, lift up your voice;
> Night and stars, in God rejoice.[11]

This was serious traditional church music, the kind I had been brought up on. Ann also wanted to find out more. So I went on ahead through the crowd and soon discovered the source. An African man sat alone on a bench, hymnbook in hand. I joined him there for the third stanza, "Men and women, young and old, raise the anthem loud and bold." People glanced and hurried by as if we were a couple of huge bugs in a Gary Larson "Far Side" cartoon.

My fellow believer was a seminarian from Nigeria. He said he had sung this way in several European depots. "Of course," he remarked, "people think I'm mad. But who knows what may happen?"

Families surviving mental illness are swelling an "anthem loud and bold." Results of the music are discussed in the chapter ahead.

10
Cheating Winter

For God alone my soul waits in silence;
from him comes my salvation.

—Psalm 62:1

Beloved, we are God's children now;
what we will be has not yet been revealed. What we do know is this: when
he is revealed, we will be like him, for
we will see him as he is.

—1 John 3:2

"Remember the Sabbath day, and keep it holy" (Ex. 20:8). The summons to stop for a day and measure our daily pressures against God's
ultimate purpose expresses a biblical reframing option. When one of
its modern outcomes—the academic sabbatical leave—came my way,
I eagerly accepted the generous offer: I could let go for almost a year's
exit from the illness scene absorbing so much of my energy.

Ann and I decided first to visit our son Brad, who had by this time
settled in Australia. Before leaving, however, we began building a
caregiver coalition—health and social work professionals, our pastor,
and friends—to support Jay in the projected eight-month absence.
The visiting scholar teaching post that opened in Brad's overseas locale added to our good fortune.

Because "Down Under" from our home on the West Coast was
practically half a world away, rather than purchasing a return trip
ticket we went instead for an around-the-world one with layover stops
allowed. Subsequently, early in the fall we headed for the East Coast,
Europe, India, and Southeast Asia. By the time we reached southern
Australia in November, however, summer was already on its way
there. Crossing the Pacific for the United States and home the next
April, something we had never thought of became apparent. Our trav-

els had always kept us one step ahead of the cold; in fact, we had bypassed a winter season during the time away.

From nature's standpoint I am sure good climatic reasons exist for winter; I cite its bleakness and cold here only as a metaphor of regrets and sadness of spirit. "Winter" threatens any long-term caregiver engaged with symptoms of challenging mental illness evident in a loved one. Still, from a history of denial, false leads, and risks, I have kept beyond the grip of frozen despair. And I anticipate "springtime" happenings will eventually support success as well.

Learning to Hope

To be honest, sometimes I feel like giving up, especially during rehospitalization periods. Nevertheless, I have experienced how grieving and feeling down are commonplace during those unpredictable setbacks. Yet reverses also prove transient when professional caregivers are at their best. In an American culture that expects the expert and specialist to have answers to various "problems," however, I should not press too far in expecting a language of religious consolation from them; I have come to depend even more on letting the Bible speak its comfort.

The professionals have not only urged me to risk more effective treatments in Jay's case, they have prodded me to take a look at *hope* potential, poised between grief on the one hand and faith on the other. I refer to advances of innovative research on the landscape of long-distance coping with chronic mental illness in the family.[1] In the "Finding Out" and "Holding On" sections of this book, I have given a family history of psychiatric *treatment* intervention (psychotherapy and chemotherapy) for a mental disorder. More than a decade has elapsed, and today a different angle of the story, namely, psychiatric *rehabilitation,* beckons our family.

Once Jay left home, we involved ourselves with a number of his community residence settings. Yet the treatment intervention here—especially chemotherapy—seemed simply to be a hospital regimen adapted to a noncustodial base. As illustrated by the anecdotes in previous chapters, our son has stayed on hold as far as social skills are concerned; he has quite limited ability to converse with family and friends, for example, and his tranquilizer medication program has evidently induced a shy apathy that puts job search and interviewing in limbo. To me he is "chronically mentally ill" as a consequence. Some rehabilitation spokespersons, however, reject the label as stigmatizing and merely an invitation to pessimistic expectations.[2] In view of what I consider mostly a physical, biological brain disease, I have my doubts about that but at the same time disclaim having the sure answer myself. I join others in also wanting to learn more.

A brief overview of initiatives set forth by the proponents of psychiatric rehabilitation begins with a look at the past. The help we got from the Rose Club at Pacific Community Mental Health Center supports emerging research data from other parts of the country. Both clients and their families have benefited from respite support and by cultivating an attitude of hope. Psychosocial rehabilitation centers like Portals House in Los Angeles, Fellowship House in Miami, and Thresholds in Chicago have, with measurable success, stressed health induction rather than symptom reduction, affirming that persons with severe psychiatric disabilities have the capacity to recover better health. New York City's Fountain House has conducted national training programs for professionals, and our local Rose Club has improved its services as a result. Making this pioneering model (founded by ex-patients) serve even more effectively undergirds a vision for the future.[3] It converges with a biblical revelation: The Lord, asserts David, "redeems your life from the pit" and crowns the faithful "with steadfast love and mercy" (Ps. 103:4).

On the negative side, these researchers hold that false leads of the past (historical "myths") actually have blunted progress and must be discarded. As far as our family encounters are concerned, I cite two examples. One such myth, "Increasing compliance with drug treatment can singularly affect rehabilitation outcome," reflects the way we used to assume how Jay "would come to his senses" on medication and take up normal living once more. It dawned on us after a time that medications are simply for control of symptoms; kindling within the patient a motivation to take up college again or find employment was another matter. Furthermore, compliance with a chemotherapy program does not eliminate the risk of relapse. Thus psychiatric rehabilitation, it seems to me, has become not so much an added luxury as a necessity for any progress and healing.

Another myth these rehabilitation pioneers call to our attention arises from the present-day practice of diagnosing serious mental illness. In their view, it is wrong to suppose that a person's diagnostic label provides significant information relevant to his or her future re-habilitation outcome. The effort, it seems, can steer treatment away from the *person*. They suggest that *DSM-IIIR* fails to connect diag-nostic conclusions with adequate bases for long-term treatment plan-ning. Not enough thought is given to the environment the client needs or wishes to live within. There remains, they conclude, so much more to learn, risk, and experiment with.

Despite everything, I am still inclined to approach medical person-nel like priests of healing whose words for Jay's illness become magi-cal answers to the pain and dilemmas a parent such as I must face. I never take them lightly, for desperately I want to assume actions they initiate will control or eliminate the "problem." Yet at the same time, there is a danger that the more the professionals in the system take responsibility for life choices, the more helpless and dependent cli-ents and their caregiver families become. A subversive helplessness outlook like this also can feed the stereotyping that if one is irrational or "crazy," it follows that the thoughts and choices of a consumer diagnosed with either chronic or acute symptoms should be ignored.

In fact, many mental illness consumers are learning self-help steps and have recovered. To do so, they must protest the habits of what one researcher calls the "mentalism" in others they meet from day to day. Mentalism, for example, insists that

> People with serious illness are dangerous, unpredictable, and to be feared.
> What they say is crazy and can be ignored; as a result, they can have others decide what is in their best interest.
> Furthermore, these folks are more like children than adults.[4]

I join with others in attempting to unmask such prejudices. At the same time, however, I must admit that our family pilgrimage has re-vealed a degree of truth in each. From the "more like children than adults" item, consider an example.

It was time for another weekend outing from Jay's supervised housing setup. Social workers there had worked diligently to enable more independent living for their client. Even though these friends from Pacific Community Mental Health Center had taken him shop-ping several times and provided cooking instructions, it began to look as if he had lacked motivation enough to fix himself a decent meal for some time past.

We headed for a favorite buffet-style restaurant. I sensed Jay's enjoyment, prepared as he was for a help-yourself feast. As usual, however, silence reigned in our booth until all of a sudden my dinner companion ventured, "Have you seen someone slurp Jello?"

"No," I had to admit.

With a furtive glance about to make sure no one was looking, Jay lifted a couple of Jello cubes and "slurped" them through his lips. I was awarded with a broad, toothless grin. Childlike behavior for a thirty-something person, I'd say, yet I could not help joining his simple mirth. In the face of other episodes tempting me to bemoan my parenting fate, the challenge I see now is to cultivate a sense of humor for moments like these.

Unpredictably, Jay can also act as "grown up" as anyone else. Not long after the restaurant incident, we went department store shopping. As usual, Jay stepped out ahead of me but not so far as to lose track of my whereabouts. Suddenly I tripped and took a nasty fall. As I laid there on the floor—trying to catch my breath—Jay was the first to reach my side.

"Take it easy, Dad."

"Where does it hurt?"

"They're coming . . . you'll be okay."

(What better verbal first aid?)

Each case of mental illness is unique, I would guess, depending on the severity of symptoms in a given instance. The familiar "you never know what to expect" rings true. Accepting the reality the disabling condition represents means living with ambiguity. It also spurs the impulse to go beyond a holding pattern and venture new things.

Going Public

Today a familiar acronym spells NAMI: the National Alliance for the Mentally Ill. Organized a decade ago, this self-started parent group has grown from 57 self-help local units at its first organizing meeting in 1979 to about 950 affiliates today.[5]

At our initial meeting locally, Ann and I sensed with profound relief that we were *not alone* in this demoralizing family affair. Informal group discussion not only broke through the isolation we had felt so long but also released a bit of our pent-up baggage of guilt and shame.

Finally, we decided, the time had come to speak up in public about (1) the dearth of effective services for mentally ill relatives, (2) the stigma attached to clients and to families held to have caused the devastation, and (3) the need for justice in the allocation of public funds on behalf of these most vulnerable citizens. Helplessness, learned or real, began to release its hold on us.

The defining assumptions of NAMI (not stated in its by-laws) appear to be:

The issue involves not a "mental health problem" but a biologically based illness.

Symptoms arise from a no-fault disease.

NAMI families consider themselves as allies in treatment and rehabilitation plans.

The governmental public sector has a moral obligation to care for all citizens living in handicapping conditions, including those with mental illness.

Studies reveal that the typical NAMI member is a mother in her sixties with a son in his thirties who suffers from schizophrenia. I soon met parents with a variety of backgrounds: clergy, educators, businesspeople, a nuclear physicist, ranchers, physicians, nurses, and airline employees. My widening circle of contacts confirmed a research finding showing a membership largely Caucasian, well-educated, from middle and upper-middle income groups.[6] At a national convention I conversed with some of them. One woman's disclosure that both her teenage sons suffered from schizophrenia put my own conflict in a different perspective. I met parents whose children had died by suicide. "Our daughter disappeared for three weeks," said another father, "before we got a call from the Canadian police." I heard about a college senior—a good student and athlete—who collapsed shortly before graduation and whose hospitalization-supervised living record of over ten years since then closely duplicated Jay's.

I tried to share my experiences, too.

"But have you," I asked at a luncheon table, "ever seen someone so agitated they went through a pack of cigarettes in twenty minutes?"

"Of course!" a couple of listeners responded. (In other words, "So what else is new?")

Moments like these, at least for me, defined the support of the NAMI support group. I had not, after all, been living in some bizarre family enclave.

Invaluable emotional sustenance also translated into opportunities for action outside the home. Various networks accommodate a range of interests: Homeless and Missing, Legal Alliance, Guardianship and Trusts, and Sibling and Adult Children are examples. My focus is the Religious Outreach group through which I have participated in congregational awareness workshops, given papers at professional pastoral care conferences, and confronted stigma about mental illness. In one letter to the editor, I contested what I thought to be a patronizing and false newspaper article reference to schizophrenia. It brought a phone call from a desperate parent who had never even heard of Pacific Community Mental Health Center and its services. I challenge speakers at public gatherings—one of whom spoke of a "schizie" attitude—and have organized a university course offering in religion, "Hearing Voices: Your Neighbor Is Schizophrenic."

A clergy convocation speaker I wrote to was gracious enough to offer an apology. He replied,

> You are right; my use of the term was inadvertent. I apologize for any harm done. Thank you for calling my attention to my lapse into careless use of a term, and for informing me about Dr. Torrey's book on schizophrenia. I know better and will be more careful in the future.[7]

I hope he recognized my assertions arose not from a "victim" perspective but from one searching for the truth concerning public stereotyping of mental disorder.

The success of NAMI is reflected in another of my favored acronyms: WAPR (World Association for Psychosocial Rehabilitation). This international nongovernmental organization is concerned with the prevention and rehabilitation of psychiatric disabilities. Community-based rehabilitation guides its mission, and it seeks to utilize the best knowledge in the field. At a recent international congress, some thousand delegates arrived from fifty countries.[8]

I rejoice at signs of hope in the church. One minister writes that despite the threat they face of becoming numb from social agenda overload, believers need to consider the situation facing persons with chronic mental illness in our midst. In contrast, the "worried well" among us, he maintains, receive too much attention. Through prayer and teaching information, and by a well-considered call to such people to confront their loneliness and isolation, he helps me redefine the biblical word "redemption."[9]

The subject of demons could be a challenging topic for congregational Bible study. Well-intentioned but uninformed clergy need reminders of the potential harm they may cause by pleas for a "genuine" faith good enough for trying to cast out demons from sufferers in psychiatric wards. Chaplains are usually available for ministry with persons and family members at these times of treatment for acute symptoms.[10]

Looking back on Jay's acute episodes at the onset of his illness, I am still mystified by the rantings I heard about Satan, wizards, and even Lucifer. Demon possession, when I see it in the New Testament scriptures, has an uncomfortable familiarity.

At this point, the scholar Jürgen Moltmann offers guidance in pointing to the personal and *cosmic* sides of Jesus' healings and exorcisms. Demons belong to the scene of heavenly struggle, symbolizing the powers of destruction aligned against creation and life itself. Thus if illustrations concerning our Lord's casting out demons are seen only historically, their day is past and they have nothing to say to us now. Theologically speaking, however, they reveal the Exorcist's power over the forces of chaos. Death itself, the last enemy, will also one day submit (1 Cor. 15:26). Thus, Christians need constantly to lift this eschatological vision of hope. It beckons to us on the horizon as we pray, "Thy Kingdom come."[11]

Until then, I intend not only to cultivate trust in divine promise but also to work within worldly circles of care (figure 4).

"Going in circles" signals getting nowhere for most people. Although partly true, "circular" thinking about chronic mental illness helps protect against the false optimism and dashed hopes of linear, progressive schemes. Thus, while Jay may find a home in a congregate care facility or in supervised housing or even go back to the hospital (public or private) for stabilization, the family continues its support as an ally of both Jay and the public caregivers.[12] A change in locale is simply that; it does not have to mean a setback in the process of constantly reaching out for that elusive "progress." Reality has

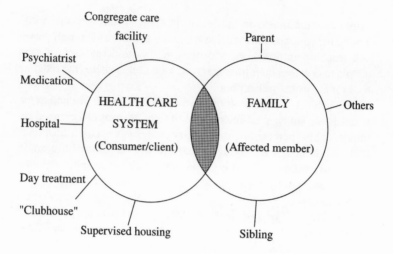

FIG. 4. CIRCLES OF CARE

taken hold; moreover, this requires parents to make will or guardian-ship arrangements to ensure, as best we can, care during our children's undefined "circular" future.

A reality like this outlook need not squelch hope. Medical break-throughs, for example, may come about. New ventures in rehabilita-tion could alter sustainable caregiving routines to accomplish increas-ingly independent living standards and authentic progress.

Going Gentle

I began my story about the appearance of mental illness in our family by citing the first symptom as I saw it: rage. Personality slowly faded in the onslaught, and an outsider began to take Jay's familiar place among us.

Dylan Thomas's words fit the scene. "Rage," cries the poet, "against the dying of the light." The last verse of "Do Not Go Gentle into That Good Night" sounds a call for resistance to the evil:

> And you, my father, there on the sad height,
> Curse, bless, me now with your fierce tears, I pray.
> Do not go gentle into that good night.
> Rage, rage against the dying of the light.[13]

Death in the family moves the poet's lament. From it I am also reminded of the sad height of the mountain in Moriah's land where Abraham was about to sacrifice his son, Isaac (Genesis 22). They "walked on together," father and son (vv. 6, 8).

Taken as Jay's words, the last stanza echoes the story of my walk with him. Yet, instead of only lamenting the dying of sanity, I prefer to reframe. The night, Thomas also reminds me, somehow is good. Rather than mere rage, I seek a pace of "going gentle"; instead of lingering by the poet's curse, I shall watch for his hint of blessing.

Abraham risked all, even his son, by trusting a promise of the future in Sarah's child. It evolved into both survival and blessing. Trust in the promise—faith—is the key. Death in the end will defeat the poet and the rest of us as well. But Dylan Thomas—like Jacob wrestling with the angel (Genesis 32)—embraces resistance first. Faith, opposition, and hope together comprise the essentials of "going gentle." On the inside, I cannot help raging against chronic mental illness, but at the same time I will admit to strange blessings in its wake. For me, the biblical words "compassion" and "patience" have become neither unfamiliar nor strange. I have learned and been changed in (1) personal priorities, (2) awareness of the public service system, and (3) spiritual insight. Let me comment on the last of these.

From a human perspective, endurance embraces hardship and tenacity. Still, endurance also covers the positive; it involves even the Lord as well. Psalm 117, a hymn of praise, reminds readers about the Bible's ultimate vision:

> Praise the Lord, all you nations! . . .
> For great is his steadfast love toward us,
>   and the faithfulness of the Lord endures forever.

(Ps. 117:1–2)

According to the biblical field of vision, the divine endurance will extend to a renewal of the Eden-like peace that reigned before chaos and death invaded our lives.

> See, the dwelling of God is among mortals.
> He will dwell with them as their God;
> they will be his peoples,
> and God himself will be with them;
> he will wipe away every tear from their eyes.
> Death will be no more;

mourning and crying and pain will be no more,
for the first things have passed away.

(Rev. 21:3–4)

Note how we ourselves cannot wipe away each other's tears; only God can do it. Until then I dream of a "next things" day when not the anorexic-looking, silent Jay appears before us but the young man we knew before the stranger took his place. We will shake hands, assure him that he was never unwanted or unloved, and he will say, "It's over."

Then, riddles and dimly lit mirrors aside (1 Cor. 13:12), we will hear his story and learn more about God and special errands.

Notes

Preface

1. Lewis L. Judd, NIMH Report, "Putting Mental Health on the Nation's Health Agenda," *Hospital and Community Psychiatry* 41, no. 2 (February 1990), n.p.

2. Don Browning et al., eds., *Religious and Ethical Factors in Psychiatric Practice* (Chicago: Nelson-Hall, 1990), 296. Robert Coles, *Harvard Diary: Reflections on the Sacred and the Secular* (New York: Crossroad, 1988), 10–12.

3. Christopher Lasch, *The Minimal Self* (New York: W. W. Norton & Co., 1984), 65–69, 94–99.

4. Robert Hughes, *Culture of Complaint: The Fraying of America* (New York: Oxford University Press, 1993), 4–10.

5. I am indebted to N. J. Robb's unpublished paper, "Pastoral Care as Witness" (St. Andrews, Scotland: St. Mary's College, 1992). An important critique of popular self-help books is Wendy Kaminer's "Saving Therapy: Exploring the Religious Self-Help Literature," *Theology Today* 68, no. 3 (October 1991): 301–25; see also her book *I'm Dysfunctional, You're Dysfunctional: The Recovery Movement and Other Self-Help Fashions* (Reading, Mass.: Addison-Wesley Publishing Co., 1992). See also Karen E. Horowitz and Douglas M. Lanes, *Witness to Illness: Strategies for Caregiving and*

Coping (New York: Addison-Wesley Publishing Co. 1992) for a nontheological viewpoint.

6. Leo Tolstoy, *Anna Karenina* (New York: New American Library, Signet Classic, 1961), 17.

7. Margaret Mantle, *Some Just Clap Their Hands* (New York: Adams Books, 1985).

Chapter 1: Rage in the Rec Room

1. The epigraph's quotation from the final verse of the Dylan Thomas poem "Do Not Go Gentle into That Good Night" is from Dylan Thomas, *Collected Poems, 1934–52* (New York: New Directions, 1953).

2. David Shore (ed.), *Schizophrenia: Questions and Answers* (Rockville, Md.: U.S. Department of Health and Human Services, 1986), 1, emphasis added.

3. See the discussion of Stephen R. Covey, *The Seven Habits of Effective People* (New York: Simon and Schuster, 1989), 104–6.

4. *The Experiences of Patients and Families: First Person Accounts* (Arlington, Va.: National Alliance for the Mentally Ill, 1989), 65–66.

5. See Harriet P. Lefley and Dale L. Johnson, eds., *Families as Allies in Treatment of the Mentally Ill* (Washington, D.C.: American Psychiatric Press, 1990). "Most schizophrenia researchers now agree that parents do *not* cause schizophrenia" (Shore, *Schizophrenia*, 9). See Nancy C. Andreasen, *The Broken Brain: The Biological Revolution in Psychiatry* (New York: Harper & Row, 1984), preface. See also Titus 1:5. In today's industrialized societies life-span expectancy stretches beyond first-century limits. Extending adolescence and age of marriage poses greater parental challenges than in eras when children left home at an earlier age. Thomas C. Oden, *First and Second Timothy and Titus,* Interpretation (Louisville: John Knox Press, 1989), 28–30, 146–47.

6. Mark U. Edwards, *Luther's Last Battles: Politics and Polemics 1531–46* (Ithaca and London: Cornell University Press, 1983), 9–19. Edwards attributes the symptoms rather to the culture of the times; many others also used scatological language for the devil, for example.

7. Walter von Loewenich, *Luther's Theology of the Cross,* trans. Herbert J. A. Bowman (Minneapolis: Augsburg Publishing House, 1976), 134–35.

8. Arthur Frank, *At the Will of the Body: Reflections on Illness* (Boston: Houghton Mifflin Co., 1991), 3.

9. Marybelle Walsh, *Schizophrenia: Straight Talk for Family and Friends* (New York: William Morrow & Co., 1985), 173.

10. Roland E. Murphy, "Modern Approaches to Bible Study," in *The New Oxford Annotated Bible, New Revised Standard Version,* ed. Bruce M.

Metzger and Roland E. Murphy (New York: Oxford University Press, 1991), 388–92.

11. Walter Brueggemann, *David's Truth in Israel's Imagination and Memory* (Minneapolis: Fortress Press, 1985), 9–11. I seek to put theology into practice in the remaining chapters. See Mark Ellingson, *The Integrity of Biblical Narrative: Story in Theology and Proclamation* (Minneapolis: Fortress Press, 1990), 18–22.

Chapter 2: A Domestic Chernobyl

1. Zhores A. Medvedev, *The Legacy of Chernobyl* (New York: W. W. Norton & Co., 1990), preface.

2. Chris C. Park, *Chernobyl: The Long Shadow* (New York: Routledge, 1989), preface.

3. See Jer. 9:15; 23:15; and see *Harper's Bible Dictionary,* ed. Paul J. Achtemeier (San Francisco: Harper & Row, 1985), 1142–43.

4. Nancy C. Andreasen, *The Broken Brain: The Biological Revolution in Psychiatry* (New York: Harper & Row, 1984), 265, 267.

5. *Harvard Mental Health Letter* 8, no. 3 (September 1991): 1–3.

6. Mary Kay Blakely, "Dangerous to Himself or Others," *Lear's* 4, no. 4 (June 1991): 48–49.

7. *The Experiences of Patients and Families: First Person Accounts* (Arlington, Va.: National Alliance for the Mentally Ill, 1989), 67.

8. Phyllis S. Vine, *Families in Pain: Children, Siblings, Spouses and Parents of the Mentally Ill Speak Out* (New York: Pantheon Books, 1982), 209–13.

9. Marybelle Walsh, *Schizophrenia: Straight Talk for Family and Friends* (New York: William Morrow & Co., 1985), 33–35.

10. E. Fuller Torrey, *Surviving Schizophrenia: A Family Manual* (New York: Harper & Row, 1988), 274.

11. Walter Brueggemann, *The Creative Word: Canon as a Model for Biblical Education* (Philadelphia: Fortress Press, 1982), 34.

12. Blakely, "Dangerous," 48.

13. Abigail Van Buren, *A Family Affair: Helping Families Cope with Mental Illness* (New York: Brunner/Mazel, 1986), 3–6.

14. Ibid., 15.

15. Patricia E. Deegan, "Accepting the Challenge to Care: The Religious Community and the Mentally Ill" (Hyannis, Mass.: National Catholic Office for Persons with Disabilities, n.d., mimeographed).

16. Leona L. Bachrach, "Hearing Patients' Words" (Paper delivered at the convention of the Association of Mental Health Clergy, New York, May 16, 1990), 3, 15. For a "case story" (vs. "case study") that examines long-

term coping from the perspective of one living with symptoms of schizophrenia, see Frederick J. Frese, "A Calling," *Second Opinion* 19, no. 3 (January 1994): 11–25.

17. Ed Cooper, "To Touch the Untouchable," Pathways to Promise (St. Louis, n.d., mimeographed).

18. Bachrach, "Hearing Patients' Words" 3, 15.

19. Carolyn Welch Griffin, Marian J. Wirth, and Arthur G. Wirth, *Beyond Acceptance: Parents of Lesbians and Gays Talk about Their Experiences* (New York: St. Martin's Press, 1986), 16.

Chapter 3: Of Cuckoos Nests
and Loony Bins

1. Num. 35:6–28; Deut. 19:1–13; Josh. 20:1–9. See "refuge" in *Harper's Bible Dictionary* (San Francisco: Harper & Row, 1985), 858.

2. The King James Version of Mark 3:19–21 reads: "When his friends heard of it, they went out to lay hold on him: for they said, He is beside himself." To be "beside oneself" is closer to the literal meaning of the Greek. The New English Bible has "they set out to take charge of him." The Jerusalem Bible reads the same and states that his family was "convinced he was out of his mind." See E. Fuller Torrey, *Surviving Schizophrenia: A Family Manual* (New York: Harper & Row, 1988), 311.

3. Nancy C. Andreasen suggests the gifted king had fallen prey to depression and despair; see *The Broken Brain: The Biological Revolution in Psychiatry* (New York: Harper & Row, 1984), 1. Western culture has a religious tradition of hospitality (see Luke 10:25–37, the parable of the good Samaritan). By the thirteenth century in Europe, the word "hospice" referred to "a house for permanent occupation by the poor, the *insane* [italics added], and the incurable," presumably sufferers from the plague and leprosy. The hospital then developed as a place where sick individuals were temporarily accommodated for medical treatment. The hospice was originally administered by a community of Christians vowed to the religious life. See *New Catholic Encyclopedia,* ed. Catholic University of America, vol. 7 (New York: McGraw-Hill, 1967), 155–58.

4. Albert Q. Maisel, "Bedlam 1946: Most U. D. Hospitals Are a Shame and a Disgrace," in *Nowhere to Go: The Tragic Odyssey of the Homeless Mentally Ill,* ed. E. Fuller Torrey (New York: Harper & Row, 1988), 1–2.

5. M. Gilbert Porter, *One Flew over the Cuckoo's Nest: Rising to Heroism* (Boston: Twayne Publishers, 1989), 14.

6. Kate Millett, *The Loony Bin Trip* (New York: Simon & Schuster, 1990).

7. Ann Braden Johnson, *Out of Bedlam: The Truth about Deinstitutionalization* (New York: Basic Books, 1990), 62–63. But Torrey, *Surviving Schizo-*

phrenia, 242–43, argues the need for asylum, as used in its original sense, for some patients having more severe symptoms.

8. *Harper's Bible Dictionary,* 80, 81.

Chapter 4: Faith and Frenzy

1. Arthur Frank, *At the Will of the Body: Reflections on Illness* (Boston: Houghton Mifflin Co., 1991), 12, 13, 119, 128; epigraph from 47 and 49.

2. See E. Fuller Torrey, *Surviving Schizophrenia: A Family Manual* (New York: Harper & Row, 1988), 321–23, for a discussion of the insanity defense. In Martin Marty, *Health and Medicine in the Lutheran Tradition: Being Well* (New York: Crossroad, 1983), illness and madness are analyzed in depth.

3. American Psychiatric Association, *Mental Illness: There Are a Lot of Troubled People* (Washington, D.C.: American Psychiatric Press, 1988), 1–3.

4. Ibid., 10–11. See also "Schizophrenia: A New Drug Brings Patients Back to Life," *Time* (July 6, 1992): 52–60. Statistics about costs from the National Institute of Mental Health are included in the discussion of the promising new drug clozapine in David Shore, ed., *Schizophrenia: Questions and Answers* (Rockville, Md.: U.S. Department of Health and Human Services, 1986), 1.

5. Susan Sheehan, *Is There No Place on Earth for Me?* (New York: Random House, Vintage Books, 1983).

6. See comments of Bernhard W. Anderson, *Understanding the Old Testament,* 4th ed. (Englewood Cliffs, N.J.: Prentice Hall, 1986), 399–410.

7. Nancy C. Andreasen, *The Broken Brain: The Biological Revolution in Psychiatry* (New York: Harper & Row, 1984), 191–93; Daniel Patrick Moynihan, "Promise to the Mentally Ill Has Not Been Kept," *New York Times,* May 22, 1989 (letter).

8. Nancy Andreasen, *Understanding Mental Illness: A Layman's Guide* (Minneapolis: Augsburg Publishing House, 1974), 11–12. See also her *The Broken Brain* for a description of psychodynamic, behavioral, and biological models used in current studies. I emphasize the latter and, in particular, the insights of E. Fuller Torrey in *Surviving Schizophrenia.*

9. Andreasen, *The Broken Brain,* 30–31.

10. Milt Freudenheim, "Seeking Safer Treatments for Schizophrenia," *New York Times,* January 15, 1992, C5. See part 4, "The War against Treatment," in Rael Jean Isaac and Virginia C. Armat, *Madness in the Streets: How Psychiatry and the Law Abandoned the Mentally Ill* (New York: Free Press, 1990), 161–247.

11. *Harvard Mental Health Letter* 8, no. 12 (June 1992): 5.

Chapter 5: Give Us This Day
Our Daily Meds

1. The Spurgeon epigraph is taken from *Context* (Chicago: Claretian Publications), March 1, 1992, 6.

2. Burton Cooper maintains that we are not to think of God's powers or abilities as simply an unlimited extension of our powers or abilities. See "The Disabled God," *Theology Today* 68, no. 2 (July 1992): 173–82.

3. Karen Lebacqz, "Imperiled in the Wilderness," in *Second Opinion*, vol. 2 (Chicago: Park Ridge Center, 1988), 26–31.

4. See Bernhard W. Anderson, *Understanding the Old Testament*, 4th ed. (Englewood Cliffs, N.J.: Prentice-Hall, 1986), 86–87. See Deut. 8:3 and also Matt. 4:4 as a counterpart.

5. *Harper's Bible Dictionary* (San Francisco: Harper & Row, 1985), 1133; the Hebrew word *midbar* suggests a wild wasteland where humans may become bewildered or disoriented. See J. J. von Allmen, ed., *A Companion to the Bible* (New York: Oxford University Press, 1958), 283–84; see Matt. 12:43; Luke 8:29.

6. John Talbott, "The MacNeil/Lehrer Report," on PBS (Public Broadcasting System), April 1, 1987. See Nancy C. Andreasen, *The Broken Brain: The Biological Revolution in Psychiatry* (New York: Harper & Row, 1984), chaps. 5–6; and E. Fuller Torrey, *Surviving Schizophrenia: A Family Manual* (New York: Harper & Row, 1988), chap. 6.

7. Numbers 11–20; Anderson, *Understanding the Old Testament*, 115.

8. Dietrich Bonhoeffer, *Letters and Papers from Prison*, ed. Eberhard Bethge (New York: Macmillan Co., 1967), 126.

Chapter 6: Exodus to Main Street

1. Phyllis Vine, *Families in Pain: Children, Siblings, Spouses, and Parents of the Mentally Ill Speak Out* (New York: Pantheon Books, 1982), 93.

2. Harriet P. Lefley and Dale L. Johnson, eds., *Families as Allies in Treatment of the Mentally Ill* (Washington, D.C.: American Psychiatric Press, 1990), 31.

3. Christopher Lasch, *The Minimal Self: Psychic Survival in Troubled Times* (New York: W. W. Norton & Co., 1984), 185.

4. E. Fuller Torrey, *Nowhere to Go: The Tragic Odyssey of the Homeless Mentally Ill* (New York: Harper & Row, 1988), 199, 206. Three axioms paved the way by the end of 1961, he maintains. They were: (1) psychiatric hospitals are bad and should be closed; (2) psychiatric treatment in the community is better because cases can be detected earlier and hospitalization thereby avoided; (3) the prevention of mental diseases is the most important activity

to which psychiatric professionals can aspire. "From that point onward it was all downhill for the mentally ill," 97; Maryellen Walsh, *Schizophrenia: Straight Talk for Families and Friends* (New York: William Morrow & Company, 1985), 134.

5. Phillip Boffey, "Advancing on Schizophrenia," *New York Times,* March 16–20, 1986 (series of four articles). See also E. Fuller Torrey, *Surviving Schizophrenia* (New York: Harper & Row, 1983), 229; and Vine, *Families in Pain.* Rael Jean Isaac and Virginia C. Armat, in *Madness in the Streets: How Psychiatry and the Law Abandoned the Mentally Ill* (New York: Free Press, 1990), 65–107, expose the vast misinformation and confusion: "The effect of community psychiatry, then, was to promote the goals of anti-psychiatry— 'liberating' patients from institutions to the spurious freedom of the streets and enslavement by their illness" (105).

6. Isaac and Armat, *Madness in the Streets,* 127, 140, 141.

7. "Report Faults Community Mental Health Clinics," *New York Times,* October 7, 1991. See also Ann Braden Johnson, *Out of Bedlam: The Truth about Deinstitutionalization* (New York: Basic Books, 1990), xvi. She examines five "myths": that the depopulation was a planned phenomenon; that psychotropic medication could cure mental illness; that mental illness was itself a myth; that the mentally ill would be better off in the community; and that deinstitutionalization would save the taxpayers money.

8. Ibid., 197–98; Walsh, *Schizophrenia: Straight Talk,* 134–38.

Chapter 7: Care in Focus

1. Timothy G. Kuehnel, et al., *Resource Book for Psychiatric Rehabilitation: Elements of Service for the Mentally Ill* (Baltimore: Williams & Wilkins, 1990), 4.

2. Rael Jean Isaac and Virginia C. Armat, *Madness in the Streets: How Psychiatry and the Law Abandoned the Mentally Ill* (New York: Free Press, 1990), 249.

3. "Questions and Our Answers," *Mayo Clinic Health Letter* 2, no. 9 (September 1993): 8, cites lithium in this case. Besides recommending flossing, fluoride mouth rinses, and saliva substitutes, the answer recommends, "Finally, ask your doctor whether your son can tolerate a lower dose of lithium."

4. Robert Frost, "The Death of the Hired Man," in *Complete Poems of Robert Frost, 1949* (New York: Henry Holt & Co., 1949), 53.

5. James G. Hanson and Charles A. Rapp, "Families' Perceptions of Community Mental Health Programs for Their Relatives with a Severe Mental Illness," *Community Mental Health Journal* 28, no. 3 (June 1992): 181–97. See chap. 6, "The Wisdom of Self-Nurturance," in Karen E. Horowitz and

Douglas M. Lanes, *Witness to Illness: Strategies for Caregiving and Coping* (New York: Addison-Wesley Publishing Co., 1992), 161–97.

6. Ami Brooks Gantt et al., "Family Understanding of Psychiatric Illness," *Community Mental Health Journal* 25, no. 2 (summer 1989): 101–8. For a program model aimed at providing relief from the threat of exhaustion, see Charles R. Goldman et al., "Providing Respite for Families of Seriously Mentally Ill Adults and Training for Mental Health Professionals: A Collaborative Model," *Innovations and Research* 2, no. 4 (1993): 19–25.

Chapter 8: Giving Sorrow Words

1. John M. Cannon, "Pastoral Care for Families of the Mentally Ill," *Journal of Pastoral Care* 3 (1990): 214–15.

2. Granger W. Westberg, *Good Grief* (Philadelphia: Fortress Press, 1962), 9. A more inclusive definition given by D. K. Switzer in "Grief and Loss," *Dictionary of Pastoral Care and Counseling,* ed. Rodney J. Hunter (Nashville: Abingdon Press, 1990), 472–75: "The complex interaction of affective, cognitive, physiological, and behavioral responses to the loss by any means of a person, place, thing, activity, status, bodily organ, etc., with whom (or which) a person has identified, who (or which) has become a significant part of an individual's own self." The term "loss" appears as the crux of the statement.

3. "Grieve," in Clinton Morrison, *An Analytical Concordance to the Revised Standard Version of the New Testament* (Philadelphia: Westminster Press, 1979), 253 (*lypeo* in Greek). See John 21:17; Eph. 4:30; 1 Thess. 4:13; Mark 3:5. See Richard F. Vieth, *Holy Power, Human Pain* (Bloomington, Ind.: Meyer-Stone Books, 1988), 5–6.

4. Nicholas Wolterstorff, *Lament for a Son* (Grand Rapids: Wm. B. Eerdmans Publishing Co., 1987), 31, preface.

5. Mona Wasow, "The Need for Asylum for the Chronically Mentally Ill," in *The Experiences of Patients and Families: First Person Accounts* (Arlington, Va.: National Alliance for the Mentally Ill, 1989), 71.

6. Jürgen Moltmann, *Theology of Hope* (New York: Harper & Row, 1967), 24–25.

7. Ibid., 32.

8. Richard Mouw, "A Kinder, Gentler Calvinism," *Reformed Journal* 40 (October 1990): 11–13.

9. William Anthony, Mikal Cohen, and Marianne Farkas, *Psychiatric Rehabilitation* (Boston: Center for Psychiatric Rehabilitation, 1990), 25.

10. Leona L. Bachrach, "Hearing Patients' Words," delivered at the convention of the Association of Mental Health Clergy, New York, May 16, 1990, 15. Anthony et al., *Psychiatric Rehabilitation,* states, "Hope is an es-

sential ingredient of the rehabilitation process," 65. The quotation is from a remarkable autobiography of recovery from serious mental illness: Carol North, *Welcome Silence: My Triumph over Schizophrenia* (New York: Simon & Schuster, 1987), 52.

Chapter 9: Reframing

1. Donald Capps, *Reframing: A New Method in Pastoral Care* (Minneapolis: Fortress Press, 1990), 17. For an example, note how King Solomon reframes the dispute of two harlots over a dead child, 1 Kings 3:16–27. See "positive reframing" in Liz Kuipers et al., *Family Work for Schizophrenia* (London: Gaskell, 1972), 32–36.

2. Viktor Frankl, *Man's Search for Meaning* (New York: Simon & Schuster, 1962), 66–67.

3. H. Preisker, in *Theological Dictionary of the New Testament,* ed. Gerhard Kittel (Grand Rapids: William B. Eerdmans Publishing Co., 1964), vol. 4, 360–61, 962–63. The term is used in John 10:20 and also in Acts, in the response of the governor of Caesarea to the apostle Paul's speech: "You are out of your mind, Paul! Too much learning is driving you insane" (Acts 26:24). See also M. Green and M. Kinsbourne, "Subvocal Activity and Auditory Hallucinations: Clues for Behavioral Treatments?" *Schizophrenia Bulletin* 16, no. 4 (1990): 617–25. Preliminary data indicate that one of the experimental conditions (humming a single note quietly) reduced the duration of auditory hallucinations by 59 percent. I reported these findings to Jay, who said he had "heard about it," evidently from someone at PCMHC. Either he neglected to try or had failed to employ this simple relief method. It illustrates frustrations of treatment toward rehabilitation.

4. For the general reader I recommend commentaries by Norman C. Habel, *The Book of Job,* Cambridge Bible Commentary (Cambridge: Cambridge University Press, 1975); and John C. L. Gibson, *Job,* Daily Study Bible (Philadelphia: Westminster Press, 1985). Since the familiar "case study" designation implies nonhuman reference, I prefer "case story" to emphasize the personal reference.

5. Walter Brueggemann, *The Creative Word: Canon as a Model for Biblical Education* (Philadelphia: Fortress Press, 1982), 72–73; Bernhard W. Anderson, *Understanding the Old Testament,* 4th ed. (Englewood Cliffs, N.J.: Prentice-Hall, 1986), 595.

6. *Diagnostic and Statistical Manual of Mental Disorders,* 3d ed. rev. (Washington, D.C.: American Psychiatric Association, 1987), introduction, xxii.

7. Erhard S. Gerstenberger and Wolfgang Schrage, *Suffering,* trans. John E. Steely (Nashville: Abingdon Press, 1980), 69–74.

8. Albert Schweitzer, *The Quest of the Historical Jesus: A Critical Study of Its Progress from Reimarus to Wrede* (1910; New York: Macmillan Co., 1961), 403.

9. See E. Brooks Holifield, *A History of Pastoral Care in America: From Salvation to Self-Realization* (Nashville: Abingdon Press, 1983).

10. Claus Westermann, *Praise and Lament in the Psalms* (Atlanta: John Knox Press, 1981), 272–73.

11. *Lutheran Book of Worship* (Minneapolis: Augsburg Publishing House, 1978), no. 242.

Chapter 10: Cheating Winter

1. See William Anthony, Mikhal Cohen, and Marianne Farkas, *Psychiatric Rehabilitation* (Boston: Center for Psychiatric Rehabilitation, 1990). "Psychiatric" refers not only to treatment but also to the *disability* engendered by the illness itself. Growing out of treatment, "rehabilitation" focuses upon improved functioning in a specific environment.

2. Ibid., 4. For a helpful discussion of terminology, see Wayne Holcomb, *Of Names and Language: A Background Paper* (Louisville, Ky.: Presbyterian Serious Mental Illness Network, 1992). The terms "chronic" and "serious" are cited there as not as useful as "challenging" and "consumer." The search continues; there may be no best *single* term available at present.

3. See chap. 6, "A Clubhouse Called Home," in Anthony, Cohen, and Farkas, *Psychiatric Rehabilitation,* 16–17.

4. Ibid., 20, 28–29. For the entire list, see 18–36.

5. Agnes B. Hatfield, "The National Alliance for the Mentally Ill: A Decade Later," *Community Mental Health Journal* 27, no. 2 (1991): 95–102.

6. Ibid., 96–99.

7. Letter to the author, October 29, 1990.

8. The congress was held in Dublin, September 26–29, 1993. For the American chapter, contact President Martin Gittleman, New York Medical College.

9. Richard C. Erickson, "Caring for the Chronically Mentally Ill," *Christian Ministry* 24, no. 5 (1993): 22–24. See Rom. 8:23; Col. 1:14.

10. In general, the "possessed" of the first century (demoniacs) lived at home (Mark 7:30; Luke 8:27), cared for by family or community members. Those not extremely violent or obnoxious were evidently permitted in public places such as synagogues (Mark 1:32). Others were restrained by guards, bonds, or stocks (Luke 8:29). Some who were uncontrollable were kept at a distance and lived in deserts or cemeteries (Mark 5:1–20; Luke 8:27). Widespread search for cures of demon possession led many to seek healers (Mark

9:38–41). Exorcists practiced an art of healing that embraced sorcery (Matt. 9:34) and magic (Luke 10:17).

Current sociohistorical theories of interpretation suggest that (1) mental illness was caused or at least stimulated by social tensions; (2) it can be seen as a socially acceptable form of protest against, or escape from, oppressions; and (3) accusations of madness and witchcraft were used by socially dominant classes as a means of social control. See Paul W. Hollenbach, "Jesus, Demoniacs, and Public Authorities: A Socio-Historical Study," *Journal of the American Academy of Religion* 49, no. 4 (1981): 567–88. The biological etiology has been discussed in previous chapters. See also the discussion in Wayne E. Oates, "Biblical Demonism and Mental Illness," in his *The Psychology of Religion* (Waco, Tex.: Word Books, 1973), 257–69. Demonology references in the Bible take an intuitive and ontological approach to human suffering. Current psychotherapeutic approaches are more empirical and observational. Both exist side by side; thus by reserving judgment about either we can avoid contentious efforts to "solve" the "problem" of Jesus the exorcist.

11. Jürgen Moltmann, *The Way of Jesus Christ: Christology in Messianic Dimensions* (Minneapolis: Fortress Press, 1993), 105–11.

12. For a summary of potentials, apart from my emphasis on the religious context, see Leroy Spaniol et al., "The Role of the Family in Psychiatric Rehabilitation," *Innovations and Research* 2, no. 4 (1993): 27–33.

13. From the final verse of the Dylan Thomas poem "Do Not Go Gentle into That Good Night." Quoted from Dylan Thomas, *Collected Poems, 1934–52* (New York: New Directions, 1953).

Scripture Index

SCRIPTURE INDEX